LET'S STAY

2GETHER

AN OLD SCHOOL GROOVE

Ramona Jones

&

Darryl (DJ) Jones

1315 FIRST PUBLISHING

ISBN: 9798559508016

DEDICATION

Thank you to my husband, who has held my heart for over thirty-five years. Honey, thank you for agreeing to take this book writing journey with me and for always pushing me to be the best I can be. Thank you for standing by my side and loving me unconditionally when I resisted giving my life to God. And thank you for your continued encouragement as we work together and walk in the steps that God has ordered for our lives.

Thank you to my daughters, Quiona and Danyal, who are always encouraging me to continue writing when I get discouraged. Thank you to my son, James, for his love and support, who no matter how old he gets will always be mommy's baby boy.

I want to give special thanks to all the couples who took the time to share with us words of wisdom for the last chapter of our book what they felt helps to keep their marriages together. You guys are awesome and appreciated.

Thank you to my father-in-law for writing the foreword and departing his wisdom. Love you, dad. Thank you to my editor and proofreader J. Berry Proofreading Thank you to Ron Holliman Photography for taking the beautiful pictures for our bookcover; Thank you to the best publisher Dany J Collins and 1315 First Publishing Company.

And last, but not least, thank you to our readers. We pray that we say something in this book that will bless you and your marriage. God Bless

TABLE OF CONTENTS

Foreword

I love, admire, and am proud to call him father-in- law (dad) and Pastor. I am honored that he agreed to write the forward for our book. I have witnessed his beautiful union for over thirty years and would be proud to follow in their marriage footsteps.

Sixty-three Years of Marriage

I will share with you some of the reasons our marriage has been successful. We are both saved, sanctified, and filled with the baptism of the Holy Ghost. We use the Word of God as our guide.

Proverbs 3: 5-6 (KJV) states, "Trust in the Lord with all thine heart; and lean not unto thine own understanding. In all thy ways acknowledge him, and he shall direct thy paths."

Matthew 6:33 (KJV) states, "But seek ye first the kingdom of God, and his righteousness; and all these things shall be added unto you."

We love God, the church, family, and others. We believe in practicing love, sharing, caring for each other, and remembering one another on holidays, birthdays, and anniversaries. We have outings for a party of two we take mini vacations. Not only do I tell her "I love you," I show her; love is an action word.

Now, let us take a closer look at just how much time we have spent loving one another:

Sixty-three years is 3,285 weeks.

Sixty-three years is 22,995 days.

Sixty-three years is 551,880 hours.

Sixty-three years is 33,112,800 minutes.

And we are still counting!

In 1955, I met a young lady, Lillie B. Stampley, who became the love of my life. We were both already saved, sanctified, and filled with the Holy Ghost when we met at a church meeting one Sunday afternoon. We exchanged phone numbers and remained in contact. In 1956, I asked her to marry me. She responded by saying I would have to ask her parents' permission. Happily, they agreed after I answered a multitude of questions to their satisfaction.

Later that year, I was drafted into the army. This did not stop us from planning a marriage that has lasted sixty-three years. Our wedding was performed by our State Bishop Lizard and Bishop W.K. Gordon at the Church of God in Christ State Temple of Eastern Louisiana on August 10, 1957. The Lord has been good to us for these sixty-three years. He has blessed us with eight children: five beautiful daughters and three sons. We have twenty-five grandchildren and fifteen great-grandchildren. Two of our sons and two of our grandsons are ordained elders, and one daughter is a licensed evangelist missionary, all in the Church of God in Christ.

We give God praise and honor for how good He has been to us.

Pastor Wilbert Jones Jr.

Preface: MARRIAGE IS A GROOVE

According to Wikipedia, groove is the sense of an effect (feel) of changing pattern in a propulsive rhythm "a pronounced, enjoyable rhythm" or the act of "creating or enjoying ...

I believe that marriage is a groove. I know the word groove is an old school word but that's OK. I'm an old school girl. Before you go any further, reread the above definition of the word groove. When I read that definition, the words that jumped out at me were sense, feel, changing, rhythm, creating, and enjoying.

Doesn't that sound just like marriage? The marriage groove isn't always going to be like smooth music. Sometimes, the groove is going to be hard rock music. So, we will need to use the keywords from that definition separately and collectively in our marriages on a daily basis if we are going to keep our grooves strong.

The key is to keep listening to the beat of your marriage. We can't listen to anyone else's marriage beat. After a while, the two of you should be able to hear the same beat. That's when you'll be able to move together to a sweet, beautiful rhythm in your own marital groove.

OK, let the groove begin.

Introduction

"Then the rib which the Lord God had taken from man He made into a woman, and He brought her to the man.

And Adam said:

'This is now bone of my bones
And flesh of my flesh;
She shall be called Woman,
Because she was taken out of Man.'

Therefore a man shall leave his father and mother and be joined to his wife, and they shall become one flesh" (Gen. 2:22-24 NKJV).

We are so excited that you chose to read our book. I'd thought about writing this book for quite some time and am glad that I had the opportunity to finish this project. However, getting my husband to participate took some work. But I wore him down and got him to write a few chapters.

I decided to title this book *Lets Stay 2gether*. I can be all deep and say, *I was praying and fasting for weeks, and the Lord gave me this title*. But that would not be the truth. The truth is, I was cleaning the house and playing music, as I always do while cleaning. I love all types of music. On this particular cleanup day, I was grooving to some old school music, and the song "Lets Stay Together" by Al Green came on. I've heard this song hundreds of times. The song was released in 1972, when I was around nine years old. Growing up in my household in the seventies, my mom loved music, so Aretha Franklin, James Brown, Tina Turner, and Al Green were heard often. But hearing this song on that particular day, the words shed a different meaning.

Al said, "Whether times are good, bad, happy, or sad, let's stay together." If you think about it, that's deep. These are not simple words. You are saying to another person, no matter what we are going through; no matter if it's good times, bad times, happy times, or sad times; whenever the time; or whatever the time, we can get through anything if we just stay together.

Let's take it one step further. This does not mean just staying together in the same house and sharing expenses because it's too hard for me to live this lifestyle without your part of the rent. No, that's not the meaning I got. The meaning I got was he found his rib, his missing piece, his good thing, bone of my bone, and flesh of my flesh. It means let's have each other's back, let's build each other up, and let's catch each other when we fall. It means I'll stand by you in good health and take care of you in sickness. I'm here with you until death we do part.

As you read through the chapters of this book, it is our prayer that we say something that will admonish you to pray together, encourage you to play together, stress to you to communicate together, inspire you to date together, embolden you to make love together, and urge you to love together.

My husband and I have been married thirty-five years. We met in middle school. Back when we were there, it was called junior-high school, and the grades were seventh, eighth, and ninth.

Now, let me stop you right there before you get all sappy. I hear some of y'all saying *awww, how sweet, they've been together since middle school.* Nope, we have not been together that long. Like I said, we met in middle school we didn't date. Heck, we didn't even hang in the same circles. Firstly, I was in the ninth grade, and Darryl was in the eighth grade. Secondly, Darryl was part of the nerd, oops, I mean straight *A* group. Me, not so much. We met in ROTC. My husband loved the class and was really serious about going to the military when he came of age. Me? Well, again . . . not so much.

I do recall classmates telling me that my husband liked me back in middle school. And I must admit, I did think he was kinda cute. But that was as far as that went. We didn't reacquaint again until years later. Now, in our thirty-plus years of marriage, we are often asked how have we managed to stay together for as long as we have. First, let me say this. I know some of you who are reading this book may have been married as long or longer than us. So, you may be able to answer "How do you have a long successful marriage?" There is not one answer to that question, so we decided to share our experiences.

We don't claim to have the secrets to having the perfect

marriage. As I'm sure you already know, there is no such thing as a perfect marriage. So, the only thing we can offer is what works for us. We are an old school couple, so some things that work for us may not work in your relationship. I understand that times have changed and people view marriage and relationships differently, now. I hear people say all the time that one-on-one and being with the same person until death do you part is unfathomable and a thing of the past.

Well, I say let's agree to disagree on that point. Sometimes, going back to the old school ways is not such a bad thing. I ask you to groove through this book and check out what we have to say. Who knows? You just might learn a thing or two.

We hope you enjoy the book. And like the song says, "Whether times are . . ." You know the rest.

Chapter 1
Dating for Marriage

A Pairing Groove

Ramona Jones

"Have You Prayed Together Today?"

"An Excellent wife, who can find? For her worth is far above jewels.

The heart of her husband trusts in her, And he will have no lack of gain" (Proverbs 31:10-11 NASB).

I used to work as a Registered Behavioral Technician working with children who are on the autism spectrum. When an RBT initially starts working with a client, we do what is called pairing. We get to know our kiddo and allow our kiddo to get to know us. We learn their likes and dislikes, what makes them happy or sad, what makes them smile, what they like to eat, what their favorite things to play with are, and what will make them act out. The list goes on.

Pairing is a practice we should use while dating. We need to pair, and we need to get to know each other. We need to know more than he's a king in the sheets, she's a boss in her world, and we are physically attracted to one another.

Dating for marriage is different from regular dating. Let me explain. When you are just regular dating, it's almost like shopping. You look around, you pick up a few items, and count up the cost of buying them. You might even put them in the basket. While you are in line, you keep looking at the items you put in your basket, and when you are next in line, you take it out. I shop like that online. I fill my cart with several items; just before I checkout, I hit the view your cart button. And before I actually check out, I have removed half the items.

Then, there is the rare item that makes it all the way home. You try it out for a while, then you return it because you already knew before you took it home that the cost was too high. Don't act like y'all don't understand what I'm talking about. Sometimes, we allow Mr. or Miss Wrong all the way into our lives, and we try to make them fit into our world.

It's just like when we ladies buy that new dress that made it all the way home. We try it on with a belt, without a belt, with high heels, with flats, and with boots. Finally, we realize this is just not the right fit for us, so we return it. It's the same way with dating;

we try Mr. or Miss Wrong out in a lot of different ways: at home alone, around family, around friends, and around coworkers. Then, we finally realize we have to return them because they were not the right fit for our lives. But that's OK, because we were just regular dating nothing serious.

Marriage dating is different. We're not shopping for random products; we've already done our research. We know what we are looking for and we find it. Now, we have to be sure that it is a fit in our world. This is the time for pairing. We should use the same principles as I used with the children I worked with in our relationships. We need to get to know each other. This is the time where we learn likes and dislikes and what makes us happy or sad. This is when we learn what makes us smile, what we each like to eat, and what we like to do.

DATING FOR MARRIAGE

Make sure you are taking time to get to know each other and not just physically.

We have to pay attention when we say we have found the person that we want to share our lives with. Yes. They look good to us physically. We are all adults, so I feel comfortable saying some of us don't wait until the wedding night to experience sex together. So, they are also making us feel good physically. But we need to talk and spend time doing activities we enjoy together. Ladies, do some of the things he likes, and make sure he reciprocates. Don't let years go by and one of you is now saying, I always do what you want to do, and you never do anything I want to do. Take the time to get to know each other.

Don't date someone who is jealous of you.

I have witnessed couples who were jealous of each other.

Not physical jealousy, but the jealousy that rears its ugly head when one spouse is more accomplished in their career than the other. Or they may be jealous because you have a better relationship with your family than they do. Watch out for petty comments that may start off as funny but later become hurtful. Remember, you are just dating; don't sweep things under the rug just to get to the marriage stage because soon, that rug will start to bulge.

Check out the relationships they have with their family.

Sometimes, when we grow up in dysfunctional families, we tend to have dysfunctional relationships. This should be addressed before we get married. If your childhood pain continues to roll over into your adult relationships, we need to know if this is something our potential mate is willing to work on, or if they are just going to say this is me. This is how I am. Love me or leave me. I know we may want to ignore the issue, but sometimes, we may have to choose the latter.

Don't hang out with couples who you have to help solve disputes every time you get together.

When you become a couple, believe me, it's hard to find good couple friends. Try to surround yourself with couples who can give you good counsel, not people who want your relationship to fail. When you go out on couple dates, hang with people who like to have fun with you and are like-minded and not people who come on the date angry with each other in the beginning or leave angry at the end. It's too draining. I like to enjoy myself, and I like to be around others who like to enjoy themselves. If you hang with negative married couples before you get married, you may think that is what you have to look forward to.

Have people that you trust and listen to.

Have someone in your life that can tell you when they see red flags. Flags that you can't see because you are in too deep. (Read what I said again. I said people who you trust and will listen to.) Not just hear, but listen. We can hear everybody; we will only listen to a few.

Make sure you know what each other's vision of marriage and family is.

Don't get married and then have that "wow" moment. Wow, you want children. I never wanted children, or I don't want to have anymore children. Wow, you're a cat person. I don't like cats; I want us to have a dog. Wow, you want a single-family home. I've always been a condo person. Wow, you want an open marriage. I'm a one-on-one person. Wow, all of your children from your previous relationship will live with us. I thought it would just be me and you. Wow, your credit score is 200. I have always had good credit.

Remember, when dating for marriage, you have to find the important qualities about that person that are not physical because the physical will not last always.

Chapter 2

I Do

A Husband and Wife Groove

Ramona Jones

'Have You Prayed Together Today?"

"Therefore, what God has joined together, let no one separate" (Mark 10:9 NIV).

Are we really ready for I do?

"Am I ready to get married? Is this the person I want to spend my life with? I dare not say the rest of my life." Most of us can't make it to year five. I remember when I was young, the older married couples would tell us, "If you can make it to year five, you're doing good." We'll talk more about that later. Back to my question.

Are we ever really ready for marriage? I'm not sure. First off, we should understand what marriage is. This is the real thing, ya'll. In marriage, you are joining your mind, body, and spirit with another human being. You two have to yoke up together to carry the load. It saddens me to see the forty to fifty percent divorce rate (American Psychological).

Marriage is a gift from God; it's good times and bad times. It's service and friendship, and it's the ability to give and accept love. Marriage is leaving and cleaving with total unconditional commitment to one another.

Marriage is not a one-day event it's a lifestyle. It's a journey down a road together that has bumps, hills, potholes, twists, turns, light rain, or hurricanes. Marriage should be a loving, understanding, accepting, learning, and teaching relationship that only involves you, your spouse, and God.

Some of us have been waiting and praying for that special day to happen in our lives for a long time. And some of us have been ducking, dodging, and running from it for just as long.

Deciding to say "I do" should be one of the most important, also one of the most difficult decisions we ever make. No, ladies and gentlemen, it's not just a piece of paper, and it shouldn't be taken lightly.

Women, we are connecting ourselves to a person who we are supposed to allow to be head of our household. We are putting our trust in him to lead the family and to protect us physically, spiritually, and emotionally.

Men, you are connecting yourselves to the person who is supposed to be your rib. (Your missing piece.) This is the person you should trust to protect you physically, spiritually, and emotionally as well.

Although in today's times we have become more liberated with the approach to marriage, one thing still remains the same. Proverbs 18:22 (NKJ) says, "*Whoso* findeth a wife findeth a good *thing*, and obtaineth favour of the LORD." The word of God did not say he who finds a girlfriend or someone to shack up with. It clearly says wife. This way, he will obtain favor of the Lord. Men, don't you want God's favor?

Genesis 2:22 (KJV) says, "And the rib, which the LORD God had taken from man, made he a woman, and brought her unto the man." The man has to find his missing rib. He has to claim what is his. He has to make sure that all the other dudes out there know. "Naw, man, that's mine right there. That's my rib."

God chose the rib bone to make woman for a reason. The rib bone protects the heart and the lungs. The rib bone is strong enough to protect, yet delicate enough to break. This bone was not taken from man's head so she could be above man, nor from his feet so that she could be beneath man, but from his side. So, once she has been found, she can stand beside him.

When a man knows that you are his rib, he will protect you at all costs. You are a part of him. You are no longer two, but have become one. So, in essence, he will not just be protecting you, but he will be protecting himself.

For the ladies.

Keep in mind, a man may know that you are his rib. But he may choose not to accept it right away. In fact, he may never claim his rib. He will continue to visit all the other rib shacks in town because he thinks he's going to find a better cut of rib than you. And ladies, stop trying to throw your rib in a rib shack that it doesn't belong in. (All you will be is just another imitation rib.)

For the men.

Please don't accept imitation ribs when you can have the real thing. Take your time and look the rib over, inspect the rib, and make sure it's a choice rib just for you. I know sometimes they can make an imitation look just like the real thing. But accept no substitutes.

This is why we have to ask ourselves if we are ready for "I do". My husband and I dated for a little over a year before he asked me to marry him. We were engaged for an additional year. That time gave us the opportunity to get to know each other and decide if we were ready to make the commitment. Marriage is a huge commitment and shouldn't be decided too quickly. We had two years together before we said, "I do." I understand that some couples are together for many more years than us before they finally marry. If you're cool with that, then I'm cool with it too. But for me, I don't believe in lifetime dating. I'm a grown woman. I don't need a boyfriend.

Two years is usually enough time in most relationships to get to know each other. During this time, we get to know some of each other's likes and dislikes. (Understand likes and dislikes will change over the years.) We get familiar with some of each other's good and bad habits. (Some habits can be changed; some we just have to deal with.) We find out what the deal breakers in our relationships are. We also get to know what makes our mate's crazy jump out. (Now, don't act like y'all don't know what I'm talking about.) We can't date somebody for two years and act like we have never been introduced to Crazy. (Well, if you don't know who or what Crazy is, I'll tell you more about him a little later.)

Yes!

It's finally happened! He has asked the big question. (Did y'all check out the fact that I said, "he asked the big question?" Remember, this is an old school groove. "A man that finds a wife." Now, don't stop reading. Like I said before, let's agree to disagree. Ladies, if you want to ask your man to marry you, to each his own.)

For some women, being proposed too is like someone casting a spell over them. I don't care what is going on in the relationship, being asked to get married changes everything. Those simple words "will you marry me" have become the international game changer. Maybe at some point, you were thinking about leaving the relationship or slowing things down a bit. You may have even seen red flags thrown out from every direction. But it seems everything changes once those four little words are spoken. "Will you marry me?" Women hear those words and sometimes all rational thinking goes flying right out the nearest window.

Before she even says yes, she's thinking about that list she made, the dress she wants to wear, where she wants to have the wedding held, which one of her friends she should choose to be her maid of honor, who her bridesmaids are going to be, and where they will honeymoon.

She said yes! You are engaged. You have a ring, and you set the date. (Keep in mind, if you don't have a ring and a date, you are not a fiancé. You are still a bae or boo.) You tell your family and your friends you are engaged as you flaunt your new piece of jewelry every chance you get so everyone can see it. You jump on social media and post "I said yes" and change your status to engaged. You start looking for wedding venues, dresses, and choosing the maid of honor and bridesmaids. You start putting the choreography together for the dance at your reception. You're excited; he's excited. All is well.

Hit the pause button.

In all the excitement, there should also be the time when reality sets in for both of you. Before we say I do is the time when we should have a talk with ourselves. We should take a moment and have a self-talk. (Yes, talking to yourself is fine. Talk it out with you. Because nobody knows you better than you.)

Say to yourselves, "Self?"

"Yes?"

"Wow! Are we really getting married?"

"Yeah, we are."

"Self?"

"Yes?"

"Have we thought this thing out, or are we just excited to be getting married?"

"Yeah, we are excited, but we thought about it. It's a good idea"

"Self?"

"What now?"

"Is there some stuff we need to workout first before we get married?" (This is where we have to give ourselves an honest answer.)

If our answer is yes, there is some stuff we need to workout first, *please*, work it out. Don't just marry in order to move past it.

This is one of the major causes for marriages not lasting. People get married when there is stuff that should have been worked out before you said I do. People, please don't get married on top of stuff. Please, allow me to give you my definition of stuff. Stuff is all the negative things in our relationships that we think we can just sweep under the rug and tuck away so we don't have to deal with them. But once someone pulls back that rug, guess what? All that stuff is still there. Don't think because you went from dating to marriage that the stuff will stay tucked away, because it won't. Stuff like this includes:

Arguing and bad feelings.

I know everyone argues, but sometimes arguments can get out of control. One person may go hard on the other and say horrible things. Don't get married on top of unresolved arguments where hurtful things were said and never resolved. Those things that were said and those bad feelings will still be in the back of your mind. Getting married does not make what was said go away, it might be a temporary fix. But the way you felt when it was said is still hanging out in your mind. When I was a kid, we would say sticks and stones will break my bones, but words will never hurt me. What idiot came up with that? Words hurt and believe me when I tell you, words can cut deep. My husband and I have been around couples who have argued in front of us and said some things to and about each other that never should be said inside their home. So, to say them outside when they were not alone was just crazy to me. We must be careful of what we say. I don't want to say something horrible to the person I say I love just to win a fight.

Cheating.

If one of you was unfaithful, don't get married because you got caught. Getting married will not make everything OK. You have to deal with the infidelity. You will need to talk about it and understand why it happened. Then, we have to forgive and move on and agree that this is something that will never happen again. I don't believe in open marriages; if I had wanted to be with more than one person, I would have kept dating. If I'm not enough for you, allow me to be free. Sorry, I'm too stingy to share. Unless that's your thing. (Remember, this is an old school groove.)

Babies outside the relationship.

If we have children already before we enter a relationship, our intended will have to learn to love our children. They are now a part of the family. However, if you are supposed to be in a monogamous relationship and one of you has stepped out and had a baby outside of the relationship, don't get married just to get past the infidelity. You can't get past a child. That child will be a part of your life forever not just until they turn eighteen and you are done. You are never done being a parent.

The escape plan.

Some of us enter marriage looking for an escape plan. Marriage sounds cool they're a good person, but do I really want to be attached to one person until death do us part? That's too much to ask for. I'll give it a year or two, then I'm out. Because I know how I am. Don't enter marriage looking for the escape plan. Either you're in or you're out.

Sorry to tell you, getting married won't make stuff OK. Marriage won't make the bad good. Marriage won't make you forget the hurt. Getting married won't make you stay if you really never wanted to be married in the first place. So, take a minute and have that self-talk first before you walk down the aisle.

OK. So, you said yes; you went through all or most of the stuff.

You've had your "self-talk," and you are engaged and heading to the alter. Like most newly engaged women, when I got engaged, I was excited. But the excitement was short-lived because of my own fears and insecurities. In the back of my mind, I started to doubt if I could actually do this. The whole idea of love, marriage, one person, happily ever after. Sorry, those things did not compute in my world. I was in unfamiliar territory. I didn't have great examples of marriage growing up. So, being married and being with only one guy for the rest of my life was not something I ever thought about and, quite frankly, it terrified me.

During this period of uncertainty, I found out that there is a difference between what people put together versus what God puts together. When couples stand before God, family, friends, and the Pastor and say those vows, we really need to pay attention to the words we are repeating.

I, ____, take you, ____, to be my lawfully wedded (husband or wife), to have and to hold, from this day forward, for better, for worse, for richer, for poorer, in sickness and in health, until death do us part. In laymen's terms, ride or die. You have to be ride or die with your spouse.

Ride or die is a term people use often. We need to ask ourselves, is it just a catchy phrase to us, or do we really mean it? Are you really a ride or die person? And are you hooking up with someone who will be ride or die for you? Sorry ya'll, but I had a lot of questions before I could say I was ride or die for a dude. Where we riding to? How long is the ride going to be? Is this ride worth my time? Why I gotta die to take this ride? (I'm sorry but a sista got questions.) Alicia Keys wrote a song called "Rock With You." She said some deep words in this song. She said if they were dead broke, no job, nowhere to live, no car, she was going to stand by her man's side. Because she was gonna rock with him no matter what.

Wait a minute. Did you pay attention to the words of that song? That's a serious commitment. She said dead broke. Just in case you didn't know, there is a difference between regular broke and dead broke. If you have money just for bills, food, and gas for the car for the week and none leftover for frills, that's plain ole regular broke. But when the rent ain't been paid, you don't have money for bills, the last of food is being cooked, and you put two dollars of change in the gas tank . . . Now, you're wondering if you will be living in the car by the end of the month, that's dead broke. That's ride or die. That's what Alicia is talking about. She's talking about marriage. She's talking about until death do us part. Because that is what marriage was designed to be.

I'm cool with the whole ride or die thing. It's OK to say you are ride or die. But make sure your spouse knows your cutoff point to that phrase. (My husband knows that there is a cutoff to my ride or die level. Sorry, but a sista ain't sleeping in no car with you.)

You can't be ride or die or rock with just anybody. (Read that sentence one more time. You can't be ride or die or rock with just anybody.) Some people don't deserve that kind of commitment. That's why we should be careful before standing before God and saying I do. You are not just making a promise and commitment to each other, but you are also making a promise and commitment to God to stay together. Now, don't get me wrong, I'm not saying stay in an abusive, unfaithful, unhappy relationships just because you said I do. Only you know when it's time to walk away.

When you got married, you promised to love and cherish one another. Not be mean and abusive. That is why I say again don't get so caught up with the ring and the thought of dressing up, doing your choreographed dance at the reception, and all eyes being on you for a day. Because as the vows clearly say, it's not just supposed to be for a day; it is until death do you part.

After the honeymoon the adjustment.

You're newly married and you're happy. Every time you look at your new spouse, you smile at each other for no reason. (Aww, that's so sweet.) You're excited over your new titles. You love saying this is my husband or wife as opposed to your fiancé, boyfriend, or girlfriend.

Women run to the DMV and the Social Security Office to change our last names. We can't wait to change our status on social media from in a relationship to married. Women spend time perfecting our new signature; we love the sound of our new name when we hear someone else say mister and misses. The sky is blue, the birds are chirping, and all is well.

Then one day, you look at your spouse; the sky is no longer blue, and the birds aren't chirping. This is when reality sets in. Oh, my God. I'm really married. Now, instead of looking at your spouse and smiling, you look at them and think. *Wow! We are married. You are really going to be here every day, forever. Forever, ever.* (Aw, come on. I can't be the only one who has ever had that thought.)

And so, the adjustment period begins. Marriage is a huge adjustment. People often say that the first five years are the most difficult. I agree. We need much patience, much prayer, and much wine (OK, maybe that last part was just me.) to make it through those first few years.

Author Gary Chapman wrote books about love languages, and Author John Gray wrote *Men are from Mars, Women are from Venus*. Every couple has to get adjusted to being married, myself included. Getting married for me was like moving to a foreign country and marrying someone who didn't speak my language. My husband and my language was not only different, I thought this dude can't be from Earth. Although my husband and I dated for a couple years before we married, I don't think we really got to know each other until we said I do. I experienced several emotions during the first few years of our marriage. I felt overwhelmed, scared, lonely, frustrated, inept, irritated, confused, excited, disillusioned, happy, grateful, disappointed, trapped, crowded, angry, and loved all at the same time. And I can't even begin to imagine the emotional roller coaster he may have been on during this time period.

Darryl and I both had to learn to live with someone who was raised differently, who had different habits, morals, goals, values, and rules. We had to get used to making time for someone else to be a part of our daily routines.

For me, it was difficult getting used to someone asking me where I was going, where I had been, and when I would be back. (Really? I'ma grown woman)

But we have to adjust. (Learning to adjust and being accountable will keep a lot of problems out of our relationships.) During the adjustment period of our marriages, we will be introduced to three very important friends who will become very significant in our relationships. We will be introduced to Crazy. (You really should have gotten acquainted with Crazy prior to marriage.) Then, there is Sybil (who is usually the wife's friend). And there is the friend that comes along with all of us. Baggage.

Let's talk about Crazy. We often meet Crazy within the first two years or less. People, please. Get to know your mate's Crazy. Don't let some new Crazy sneak up on you after you say I do and surprise you. I know we all have a little low-key craziness in us, and only we can choose whose crazy we are willing to deal with. Some of our family and friends may think our spouse is crazy as hell, and we should get out of that relationship as soon as possible.

Only we know when we are dealing with that lock you up at night, showing up to your job acting a fool, jumping out of bushes, mind control, distancing you from family and friends, psychotic kind of crazy. (Don't act like you don't know the type.) Or do you just have plain ole run of the mill, mild-mannered crazy? They might have a mild tick, and they are just a little off. But they can be controlled. You have to know the difference. Please get to know Crazy.

When Darryl and I first started dating, he seemed to always get into arguments with people when we went out, and he cussed way too much. I remember saying to myself *this dude is crazy.* And even though he never argued or cussed at me, when I would hear the anger in his voice, it would make me very uncomfortable. So, I wasn't sure if that was the crazy I wanted to deal with. So, I talked to him and explained that because I grew up in a home where there was fighting and cussing often, I did not want that in my adult life. He chose to make a change for me. He didn't want to make me feel uncomfortable.

Remember, we are adjusting and getting to know each other. During Darryl and my adjustment period, I had to tell myself daily, *Girl you are somebody's wife; you said I do. Y'all not just playing house anymore; this is the real deal. Your world has changed to add another person in.*

Before we get married, we always think we are ready to share our lives with another person. Living with another person daily under the same roof is an adjustment. An adjustment that doesn't happen overnight. I had my own apartment when my husband and I met. He was just getting out of the military. After he moved into my apartment, getting used to a man in my space daily was one of the most difficult things I ever had to do. Sharing my space with another adult was hard. I had to share my bedroom, my closet, my drawers, and I'm not sure how we made it through this one. But I had to share my bathroom. Those moments of seeing toothpaste squeezed in the middle, dental floss hanging over the trash can and not all the way inside, and toilet seats being left up. In the bedroom, he kept his shoes lined up and one set of clothes folded up on his side of the bed instead of in the closet. (While writing this, I'm taking deep breaths thanking God for taking us through it.) And these are just a few adjustments we went through. I'm sure he has a list he could mention, too. But sorry, honey, this is my chapter.

During the time of adjustment, you may wish you and your spouse had different households and just hooked up when you felt like dealing with each other. Don't freak out it's a normal feeling. Adjusting takes time. During this time, there will be love, hate, laughter, tears, thoughts of staying, thoughts of leaving, thoughts of murder, and a whole lot of prayer. This adjustment time will also be the time for first-time introductions or reintroductions. This is the time when we meet those friends I was talking about earlier, Crazy and Sybil.

I got to see what would make my husband's Crazy come out for a visit. Like I already said, know your spouse's crazy. Is it run of the mill or psycho? I met Darryl's Crazy and I decided I can deal with him… And he was introduced to Sybil. The movie *Sybil* came out in the seventies; it portrayed a young woman with multiple personalities. Although there have been several movies that have portrayed individuals with multiple personalities since the seventies, I believe *Sybil* was the first movie like this I ever watched.

(Heads up to my men.) Men, at some point in your relationship, you must be introduced to Sybil. It is an absolute must, for any relationship to last. This introduction must be made. I hope you get to meet her early in the relationship. In fact, just like Crazy, I hope you make her acquaintance before you say I do.

Ladies, if you can make it through the first five years of your relationship without your husband meeting Sybil, I applaud you. And I encourage you to write a book on how to keep her in check.

I was having lunch with a friend recently who was in a fairly new relationship, and I asked her, has he met Sybil yet? She started to laugh because she knew right away whom I was referring to. She responded, "Yes, he's already met Tracy, Stacy, and Stephanie." (Now, we all know that at least one of those personalities is crazy as hell.)

Now, back to what I was saying. My husband had his first introduction to Sybil during our adjustment period. I can tell you exactly what he did to make one of those ugly personalities jump out and demand an introduction. You may think it would be something big to set her off and make her jump out and show out. But it wasn't. Y'all, it was something as insignificant as a bag of chips. My husband was going to the store and asked if I wanted anything. I said, "Yes, I would like a bag of chips." Now, anyone who knows me, knows that I love Lay's Barbeque Chips.

But on this beautiful, quiet day over thirty years ago in Los Angeles, California, my husband decided to bring back a bag of plain Lay's chips. I tell you, that personality jumped out and showed out so bad she shocked me. I tried everything in my power to reel her back in, but that girl took control. She acted a complete fool. I was ashamed of her. (But how dare he bring her plain chips?)

I know y'all think that was a stupid argument. And I agree, it was pretty stupid. But that one insignificant thing caused a bigger argument because we were still adjusting. A small problem became a big problem. We went from zero to one hundred in minutes. The argument went from you bought the wrong chips to you don't really know me at all, and if you don't know me, you can't possibly care about me. Because if you knew me, you would pay attention to my likes and dislikes. I know what you like, how could you not know what I like? It was crazy, but that is what Sybil will do. She will jump out there and show her butt and cause all kinds of problems.

Sorry guys, sometimes when Sybil jumps out, she wants to show out and not play by the rules of your marriage. It's like the old song Monica sang "Just One of Those Days."

That was not your loving wife who was lashing out at you. It's them. The other personalities. They just take over sometimes; they're the mean ones, not us.

When my husband and I were young in our marriage, when Sybil would take over, and I would become moody and would snap at him for no reason, his automatic response would be to snap back at me. But as time goes on in our marriage, we should start to adjust to each other. Ladies, we learn that, yes, we can control Sybil. We are the dominant personality. Not everything that comes to our minds has to be said. (I had to learn that lesson myself. If I thought it, I said it. Not always a good idea.) Men, you will have to learn whether to respond, ignore, or try to soothe Sybil. It's all an adjustment.

Deuteronomy 24:5 (NLT) states, "A newly married man must not be drafted into the army or be given any other official responsibilities. He must be free to spend one year at home, bringing happiness to the wife he has married." When I read this scripture, it tripped me out. Did you read what it said? The Bible gives the man a whole year with no other official responsibilities, other than to get to know his wife and bring her happiness. (Gurl, can you imagine? Your man's main responsibility for an entire year is to bring you happiness. Sign me up.) Unfortunately, we don't get that year. There is no step-by-step rulebook or Google page for every scenario that may occur in our relationships. We have to figure it out as we go.

As we begin to grow in our marriages and get to know one another, men will begin to understand that women have lots of different moods. These moods come from monthly periods, pregnancy, and other hormonal issues. We have job stress, children stress, family stress, and husband stress. And some days we just straight out feel like being a witch. (Ladies, don't let moodiness last for days. No one wants to deal with a messed-up attitude daily.)

Men, you should know when your wife is happy, sad, worried, stressed, depressed, or like I said, simply being a witch for no particular reason. Sorry guys, I don't have any warning signals for you. Like I said, attitudes sometimes just jump out and take over. Ladies, never allow your moods and attitudes to get to the point where it's considered abusive. Like I said, you can control Sybil; if you can't get control, you need to seek out some professional help. Men, get familiar with all of your wife's personalities. If you love your woman, then get to know her.

Although most women have the Sybil trait, some men have

a few personalities hanging around just dying to jump out as well. Ladies, just like us, our husbands have work stress, family stress, wife stress, head of household stress, and just being a man stress. So, when he snaps at you, don't be alarmed. Give him a moment. Don't make it about you. Men handle stress differently than women. Most men come home from work and need to relax and unwind before they want to talk about their day or about your day or what the kids did or what they need.

But women will come home from work and want to start sharing about our day, talking about our coworkers, what the kids did, or what they need. Women can work, go to school, take care of the family, and keep going. Ladies, it's cool to let him unwind from the day, but make sure you take time to unwind also. We often get so busy taking care of everyone else that we forget about ourselves.

Now that you have had the pleasure of meeting Crazy and Sybil, I may as well introduce you to Baggage.

Baggage is a sly character. Baggage is like your ghetto friend. (We all have that one ghetto friend. Both men and women.) That friend that says, *I don't care where I am, or who I'm with, I'm just gonna be me. I gotta do what I gotta do. And I gotta say what I gotta say. Love me or leave me, baby, because this is who I am.*

Baggage is just like that. It doesn't care what stage of the relationship you are in. When Baggage wants to unpack itself and act up, you better look out and pray that your marriage can survive. I'm not going to paint a pretty, perfect picture about marriage. Marriage is hard work. When it comes to Baggage, we sometimes have to ask ourselves if we are willing to hang in there for the long haul. I have witnessed Baggage take down what I thought were solid marriages.

We all bring Baggage into our relationships. Sometimes, we may not even realize what baggage we have packed away until the bag pops open. Then we have to deal with issues like trust, fear of depending on another person, I hate the way I look, intimacy issues, fear of marriage, exes, children, parents, and the list goes on.

In marriages, we get to see our spouses' strengths, weaknesses, and personal habits. But we also get to see the baggage they have packed up and brought along into the marriage.

During the first few years of our marriage, one of my bags popped open. I say one because as the years went on, several more would open up from both of us. This particular bag that decided to pop open was over packed and contained a full-blown wall. For me, this wall wasn't Baggage, it was a part of me. I loved my wall it kept me safe. My wall kept me inside and kept others out of my space. I ventured beyond my wall every now and then, but I always found my way back behind it. It was my safe space. However, during the adjustment period of our marriage, I had to get used to someone venturing behind my wall and being in my space.

(PDA) Public displays of affection I could not stand it. So, I unpacked my baggage and put up my wall of no PDA. But my husband didn't care about my protective wall. This man hugged, kissed, touch my leg, squeezed my butt, rubbed my face, and held my hand every chance he got. This was an area that my wall protected me from. And there was my husband entering into my safe zone, being his overly affectionate self. I was like, *Oh my god, could you just not touch me for a minute, please.* I know it sounds mean, but I was not an affectionate person when we first married. I didn't invite him behind my wall; he just pushed his way in.

To this day, my husband is still a very affectionate man; he grew up in a family where saying I love you and hugging was the norm. This was foreign waters for me. Not saying my mom never said she loved us. She did. But my husband was on another level. Every time he walked in a room where I was, he had to kiss me or hug me or touch me in some way. I was overwhelmed by it all. It was too much. I felt that everyone has an invisible circle around them. Others should only enter that circle when invited. (Dude broke all my "me space" rules.)

It took time for me to get used to all the public displays of affection, the hand holding, the saying I love you every day, and calling just to see how I'm doing and how my day is going. (Really! Who does that?)

All of it made me feel uncomfortable. I wanted him to stop. But that was something he would not give up on. He would not give up on me. He was determined to tear down the wall that I had built around myself and my heart for protection. He wanted to help me unpack that bag.

Keep in mind, I said help. He couldn't have just wanted me to tear down my wall. I had to want it to be torn down. I had to be a willing participant. This was not easy. That wall had kept me safe for years. It was my wall of protection. But I had to allow the chipping process to begin. It didn't happen overnight; it was exactly what I said, a chipping process. He couldn't just come in with a bulldozer and knock my wall down all at once, it was a process.

This is why we all need to take a look in our bags and find out what we have packed away. Those bags are filled with things like insecurity, jealousy, feeling distant, inability to trust, low self-esteem, low self-worth, bossiness, nit picking, I'm not good enough, I have no friends, my mom or dad left me when I was young. I could go on and on. These things can become baggage for us. We have to deal with and understand why we have these feelings. Most of the time, we go through life thinking that we are OK. We think our little baggage is nothing compared to someone else's bag. But once someone spots some of our baggage hanging out of the bag and points it out to us, we get mad or defensive. I know it's hard to face our own baggage, but there comes a time when we have to confront our own issue. Every negative thing that happens in our lives is not devil or someone else's fault. We need to do self-evaluations on a regular basis. Only then, can we make a decision to unpack the baggage so that we can stop carrying it around from place to place and relationship to relationship.

When your spouse gets a look at what's inside of one of your bags, it's up to them to decide whether or not they want to help you unpack it. If either of you chooses not to unpack, keep in mind, all through the relationship, those bags will continue to pop open. And if you never deal with the baggage inside, it can become very problematic for the longevity of the relationship. It's all an adjustment period, and it's not something that happens overnight. The unpacking process can take weeks, months, and sometimes years; it depends on how many bags each of you have and how much you have stuffed inside.

But we most know that we have to deal with it, because baggage can drive us to make rash decisions like divorce. Don't give up so fast on your marriage. I have noticed lately that people marry and divorce before the ink is even dry on the marriage certificate. If we see anything we don't like in our marriage, the first thing we say is, "I can't take this. I don't have to deal with this. They got me twisted if they think I'm putting up with this. I don't need this, I'm out." But I need you to remember what I said about the beginning of marriage. Your first few years of marriage may be a struggle. You might wonder what the heck have I done. Marriage shouldn't be this much work.

Sorry to disappoint you, but marriage is work. Let me say that again just in case you misread it the first time. Marriage is work. It is a twenty-four seven job that you are the manager of. I say twenty-four seven because even when you are not together, you have to conduct yourself like you are married. I would never want to show up to my husband's job and hear people say they didn't even know he was married, and some other women is being referred to as his work wife. Gurrl if Sybil were to hear that, I would have to hold her back. She would be in my head saying. *"oh, so they don't know you married?"* You know she is out of control. I couldn't allow her to embarrass us in public. *(smile)*

When we enter marriage for the right reason and want a loving, long-lasting relationship, we must know it won't always be easy. You'll occasionally question your judgment. But if you love each other unconditionally and keep God as the foundation, the decision you made to marry this person will be the best decision you ever made.

Chapter 3

LOVE

A Love Groove

Ramona Jones

"Have You Prayed Together Today?"

"Love is patient and kind. Love is not jealous or boastful or proud or rude. It does not demand its own way. It is not irritable, and it keeps no record of being wronged. It does not rejoice about injustice but rejoices whenever the truth wins out. Love never gives up, never loses faith, is always hopeful, and endures through every circumstance" (1 Corinthians 13:4-7 NLT).

Love.

The simple four-letter word that carries a lot of power. Do people really marry for love anymore? People get married for so many different reasons for companionship, having children together, financial reasons, having been together for all this time, they are not getting any younger, to make cute babies, to look good together, to make a great power couple, etc. But does anyone actually marry for love anymore?

We must first understand the meaning of love. Love is an intense feeling of deep affection. The feeling of deep romantic or sexual attachment to someone. According to Dictionary.com.

Love is not just a feeling. It is not always romantic.

When I was a kid, I would always ponder the word love, especially when it came to relationships. Unfortunately, my parents' dysfunctional relationship did not demonstrate a lot of love for us growing up. And all TV offered me was a fairy-tale life that I always thought I could never have.

Sometimes, we think of love as two people looking into each other's eyes, holding hands, and walking off into the sunset. Love is not a romantic comedy. There is no one there to feed you the correct lines or say cut if you say the wrong thing. There is no breaking up in the middle of the film to finally realize they are the only one for you, then finding them again to confess your undying love and live happily ever after. The End. Love is having each other's backs when times get hard. Love is taking care of each other when one is sick. It's building each other up when one is feeling down. It's pushing one another when they feel they can't go on. Love is still loving you when you are at your worst. Love is giving each other space without getting into our feelings. No, love won't always be romantic, and no, there will not always be flowers and love poems. But one thing love should always be is unconditional.

Love is respect.

Respect is so vital in our marriage. If we can't respect our own spouse, we make it difficult for others to respect them. Personally, it makes me very uncomfortable to be around a couple when one spouse is being disrespectful to the other. I almost have to bite my tongue off to not say something to the disrespectful partner. And sometimes, that does not work; I say it with a bruised tongue and all.

Love is action.

Don't just tell me you love me; show me you love me. No one wants lip service. Put love into action. If we say we love someone, we should want to see them happy. Do what you say you are going to do. There is nothing worse than someone committing to do something for you, and at the last minute, they back out. Or they say they forgot. Or worse yet, they tell you, *Oh, I didn't think it was that big of a deal.* We have to put love into action. Anyone can say they love you. In fact, people use the word so loosely now, that sometimes, I just want to ask if all of us are going by the same definition.

Love helps make life easy.

We should do the things that are within our power to make our spouse's life a little easier. In our home, I pack my husband breakfast, lunch, and snacks for work every day. And although, as I write this book, my stay at home mom days are over, and I work a full-time job every day, I still do this for him. I do this because I know packing my husband's lunch makes life easier for him. He doesn't have to think about what he is going to eat for breakfast or lunch every day. I also make life easier for myself because I don't have to worry that he didn't eat at all because he got so busy and didn't feel like going to buy something. Nor do I have to worry that he ate something too unhealthy. Darryl knows that filling my car up with gas and washing it makes my life easy. I don't have to get in my car Monday morning and have to go to the gas station, and it's nice and clean (despite the four pairs of shoes and five sweaters I have in the back seat).

Love should be reciprocated.

I don't care how much you love a person; you can't make them love you back. (Now say it with me slowly. I cannot. Make someone. Love me.) When I first heard the song "I Can't Make You Love Me" by Bonnie Raitt, I said it was the deepest song I had ever heard. It was heart-wrenching. I see so many people who want love, but they are in relationships with someone who is not in love with them. I just want to grab them and shake them and scream at the top of my lungs. YOU CAN'T MAKE THEM LOVE YOU. But on the flip side of the coin, if you continue in a relationship where you are not getting reciprocity, that means you have decided that a one-sided love affair is enough for you. If that is your decision, I still love you. God bless. But what I will say to you is, it's OK to vent occasionally, but you don't get to complain about your relationship to people every time you talk. You stayed in it.

Love is being vulnerable.

This is a very difficult requirement for some of us. Showing our vulnerabilities is challenging. Because most of us are always guarding our hearts, we won't allow ourselves to be vulnerable. I was very guilty of this. But with the right person, it's such a great feeling to let down our guard. Love will also cause our mates to guard our hearts for us. Meaning they won't do anything intentionally to hurt you, nor will they allow anyone else to hurt you. We all have vulnerabilities. We all have fears. If we love someone enough to be that transparent with them to the point that we will share some of our fears, that's huge in a relationship. Being vulnerable means that we must have a certain trust in this person. Sometimes, relationships move fast, and we share too much too soon. Sharing our feelings and fears with someone is not easy, so there has to be more to the relationship than, *We had a good rump in the hay, so we are now compatible.* Don't be so open and vulnerable with everyone. Some will help you make that vulnerability a strength, but some will prey on it

Love causes you to give one hundred percent when your spouse can only give zero percent.

Let's keep it real. There is no such thing as fifty-fifty in marriage. Things happen that are out of our control. And because of the vicissitudes of life, one of you will always have to carry a bigger load at some point in the marriage. On a daily basis, we have so many changes happening in our lives. We never know what's going to catch us off guard. In those times, one of us must be ready to give one hundred percent because our mate has nothing to give. I remember when my mother got sick with cancer. I became her primary caregiver. We tried to manage her cancer and her diabetes' levels, so it seemed like we had doctor's appointments, blood tests, or chemo every day. Some days, my mom and I would go get blood drawn and to one doctor in the morning, have lunch, then go to chemo. It was exhausting.

At those times, I had nothing to offer my husband at the end of the day. I was mentally and physically exhausted. My husband would get off of work, pick up or cook dinner, run my bath, and rub my back until I fell asleep. I didn't have anything to give, not even conversation. He had to pick up the slack. He was giving one hundred percent with his love and understanding.

Love is touching.

Touch each other. I had to come to understand this myself. Touch is very important in a relationship. Not just touching in bed, although that's a wonderful touch as well. But I'm referring to holding hands, hugs, and kisses just because. I was recently over to my in-laws. My father-in-law was sitting at the dining room table, and my mother-in-law was still asleep when we got there. When she walked into the room, she went straight to him and held his hand and said, "I missed you." And he gave her the biggest smile. I said to myself, that's the kind of love God speaks about in the Bible. Sixty-three years, and they still flirt and hold hands. That's creating a bond. My husband and I never leave the house without saying I love you and two kisses on the lips. I don't know how the two kisses started, but that's what we do. Like I said before, my husband loves PDA. Me telling my husband not to touch me, is like me telling him not to breathe. It's impossible.

Love is serving each other.

When I'm not working outside of the home, I usually cook and clean during the week. I have dinner cooked, picked up, or ordered by the time Darryl gets home. Now remember, this is an old school groove. So, I don't mind fixing my man's plate for him. But my husband knows that at a certain time of night it all shuts down, just like work outside the home. Work at home is the same; I'm off at a certain time. The kitchen is closed. Don't tell me you're hungry or you don't feel like getting your own snack. Sorry, you are on your own, dude. Now, this is not to say that he doesn't get up to serve himself and serve me during the week. But most of his cooking is reserved for the weekends. I rarely cook on the weekends. If he does not cook, he has to take me out. We must serve each other. As I said earlier, I make his lunch, and he pumps my gas. How do you serve your mate?

Love never feels alone.

In a marriage, you should never live under the same roof and feel alone. Don't live like strangers. Maybe it's just me, but I have never understood couples who vacation apart. I have always wanted to travel to Italy. I can't imagine being married and traveling to such a romantic place as Italy with my girls. It OK to have trips with our friends, but all our trips should not be us traveling as if single. If one spouse has a fear of flying or cruising, then I suggest you take a roadie. Make it comfortable, rent an RV, and take a trip together.

You should never feel alone when it comes to making major decisions. If they love you, they should be there for you. If you need to bounce your ideas off your spouse, they should be there to listen. When it comes to things like rearing the children, paying the household bills, and other major decisions, we should never feel like we are in our marriage alone.

Love includes each other in your plans for the future.

Don't say I. Say we. Not mine, say ours. This is teamwork. We are trying to build a future together. When we hear our mates talk about things to come in the future, make sure that we are hearing our name as part of the plan. I want to know that when Darryl sees himself five, ten, fifteen, twenty years down the road, if the Lord is willing, he sees me beside him.

Love is building up your spouse, not tearing them down.

How can you say you love someone if you are constantly tearing them down? Love won't allow us to point out all the negatives about our mate. No one is perfect. Love won't allow us to curse each other out and call each other out of our names. I have heard couples say that they got into it with their mate and went hard on each other. They then repeat to me the horrible things that

they said. In my mind, I'm thinking this can't be love. I get angry,
too, but I would never cut someone I love with words. Love
doesn't get around others and say my wife is dumb or that my
husband is a loser. That's your dumb wife and your loser husband.
Why tear them down? Try building them up. If your wife or
husband doesn't understand something, try and explain it in a
different way and see if that will help. Sometimes, when my
husband is trying to explain something to me, I tell him to explain
it to me like a third grader.

Love is a love song.

Every couple should have "their song." Every time you
hear your song it should make you think about your mate. My
husband and I have a few songs. My songs are, "You're Still the
One" by Shania Twain and "The Truth" by India Arie. My
husband's songs are "Through the Years" by Kenny Rogers and
"Share My Life" by Kem. I love it when my husband plays one of
our songs, grabs my hand, and pulls me into his arms for a slow
dance while he sings to me. (Well, I told y'all we were corny.)
Both of you should know what your songs are. If you only listen to
gospel music, that's OK. Your song can be something like "Never
Would Have Made It" or "I Get Joy." I ask you today. What's your
song? If you don't have one, today is the day to choose one.

Love is good loving.

Let's keep it real. There is almost nothing better than some
good loving. Nobody wants forced, obligatory loving. Anybody
can have sex. But love makes you have good, passionate loving.
When you really love someone, your focus is to please them. I
don't want my husband to come to bed and say it's Tuesday, so
let's do this. I would rather him say, "I've been thinking about
having you all day."

And ladies, I'm sure your husband doesn't want you to be like Miss Cilie from the movie *The Color Purple*, and just lay there while Mr. does his business. If you are not enjoying making love to your spouse, then y'all doing something wrong. It's time to have a conversation. Any problem can be fixed as long as you are willing to discuss it and come up with a solution together.

I leave you with 1 Peter 4:8 (NKJV) "And above all things have fervent love for one another, for 'love will cover a multitude of sins.'"

Chapter 4

TRUST

A Trustworthy Groove

Ramona Jones And Darryl (DJ) Jones

"Have You Prayed Together Today?"

"Trust in the Lord with all your heart
and lean not on your own understanding;
in all your ways submit to him,
and he will make your paths straight"
(Proverbs 3:5-6 NIV).

God is the solid foundation that holds a marriage together. Without this solid foundation, the relationship will come tumbling down. Trust is a part of that solid foundation. If you don't have trust, it will be impossible to build on the foundation. You have to gain each other's trust and try not to ever break the trust bond.

From DJ. It is so important to value the trust that you have built in your relationship. Trust is the currency of your relationship. Trust gives you the confidence to believe that you are committed to keeping your vows to each other. Once the trust has been built and developed, it is important to place a high value on it.

When I first married Ramona and I got ready to go somewhere, I would tell her, "Babe, I am going to get a haircut, and then I am going to play basketball. I should be home around 5 pm or 6 pm." The reason I did this was so she would know where I was. I made sure that I was where I said I was going to be. If the guys decided to go get something to eat, I would call and let her know.

Some of my friends would say, "Man, I guess you have to check in with your wife?"

I would tell them, "No, I don't have to check in, but my wife is concerned about me, and I want her to know that I am alright." I know my wife appreciated me being where I said I was going to be. I have always valued the trust that we have for each other, and I never want to violate or damage that trust.

Thanks for sharing that, honey. Now, back to what I was saying. Once the trust bond has been broken, it is difficult to get it back. (But not impossible.) When we enter marriage, we should ask ourselves, "Can I trust you with the very intricate details of my life?" Do I trust you enough to make decisions regarding myself, my children, finances, spiritual beliefs, and the way the household functions?

When Darryl and I started dating, I was a single mother of a four-year-old daughter, so when we started getting serious, I had to ask myself if I trusted this man. Do I trust him to make decisions regarding my life? Did I trust him to be around my daughter? Did I trust him to make decisions regarding our finances? Did I trust him to take over the role as head of the household?

I turned sixteen in October, and my daughter was born in December. My daughter and I moved out of my mother's house when I was barely seventeen. It was a struggle being a young mom on my own, but I made it happen. When I married, I had to trust that someone else could take over that head role in our lives.

My husband had to trust me as well. Would I be a good wife, mother, and friend? Or would I be the type of wife that he would hear rumors and drama that involved me, the type of drama that would embarrass him or myself.

Trust issues are baggage for some of us. This can be an issue for both husband and wife. If you had trust issues in past relationships, they can very well carry over into your marriage. These issues are usually seen before we say, "I do." However, some of us are under the false illusion that once we say I do that, our trust issues will disappear. Nothing can be further from the truth. Remember, I already told you that Baggage can stay hidden longer than Crazy.

Baggage can stay hidden so long because sometimes we don't realize it's an issue. We may not even know we have trust issues until our spouse does something remotely close to the issue that caused us to mistrust in our past relationship. We then begin to compare our spouse to our ex-relationships.

The first thing we tell ourselves is, "I'm not going through this same stuff again. I knew I couldn't trust anybody." This causes us to put up a wall to protect ourselves. (Remember my wall?) Behind our protective wall is where all of our fears and insecurities come flooding in. Behind our wall, we don't have to put up a brave front. We can sit behind our walls and talk ourselves out of trusting someone who really never gave us reason to not trust them.

Trust is something that has to be earned. There is no formula that will guarantee us that someone will never betray our trust. We have to understand that just because we are a trustworthy person does not guarantee us that you will marry someone trustworthy. Trusting the person, we have committed our lives to is a choice we have to make. We have to choose to trust them until they give us a reason not to.

In marriage, we have to make trust a priority. When you trust your spouse, you won't put them in a group or category. We really have to stop grouping all men or all women in the same categories. All men are not dogs; they don't all lie, and they don't all cheat. If your partner has never lied to you and never showed you any of the characteristic of a cheat, then get that out of your mind. Yes, he is a man. But guess what. He can be a man that is faithful to just one woman.

Men, all women are not trying to play you. We are not all conniving. We really want to be a good, trustworthy wife to a good, trustworthy husband

When we are in a relationship where trust is a priority, we should never have to ask questions like "Why didn't you answer your phone when I called?" or "Who were you with?" just because they were a little late coming home. We don't have to become private detectives and search through each other's cell phones and social media pages.

DJ. Trust is a beautiful thing. My wife has access to my cell phone, as a matter of fact, I have her facial recognition set up on my phone. Why? I have nothing to hide and want to be transparent with her.

There he goes jumping in again. To continue, as women, we usually go hard for our relationships. Nothing and no one is priority over our man. Friends, family, and sometimes children, come second. We want to show our man that we are down for him and he can trust us. We want to get into his head, know his thoughts, his hopes, and his dreams; we want to trust him enough to share our hopes and dreams. We want our husbands to encourage us to follow some of our dreams.

Most men go into a relationship protecting themselves; they never want to appear vulnerable or weak. They don't trust easily. Be patient. Give him some time. Allow him to start sharing on his own. He will open up a little bit at a time. He wants to see if he can honestly trust you; he wants to know that the things he shares with you will stay with you.

It is also important that the vulnerable things that we share with each other never be used against each other during arguments. When your spouse tells you something in confidence and you use it as a weapon to hurt them during an argument, believe me, it will be a long time before your spouse will trust you enough to share anything else for a while. If ever.

Women like to talk; we like to share our feelings. We want our man to know everything we are going through. Most men, not so much. It may take years into a relationship before most men feel comfortable enough with us to open up completely. This does not mean he doesn't love us; he just has to be sure that he can trust us.

Men are taught all their lives to man up, don't be a punk,

not to cry, and don't share your feelings because it makes you look weak. But as women, we want our mates to talk, open up, and share their feelings. We love to ask the dreaded question: *"What are you thinking about?"* My husband would always make the joke, *"If I wanted you to know what I was thinking, we would be talking."*

Ladies, back up a little from trying to get him to open up and share. But never back away. It is our job to gain our man's trust. This is your dude; he belongs to you. You chose to marry him, so it is imperative that you have his trust. Once he knows he can trust you, there shouldn't be anything he wouldn't do for you. Once he opens up to you his innermost feelings and his fears, you may be stuck with him for life. Most men will do whatever they have to do to keep you in their lives because he doesn't want to start that process over again, it's way too much work for him.

Now, let's be clear about something. At some point in our lives, someone we love will abuse our trust. That's usually a crushing feeling when the trust bond has either been damaged or broken. In a marriage, only you can decide if that bond can be repaired, no matter what the erroneous doing was. It does not matter if your family and your friends think you are out of your mind to consider building trust with that person again; it's your choice. No one can make that decision for you.

In a marriage, if trust is continually broken, it will eventually become hard to reestablish. You may even lose respect for your spouse. They may have broken the trust in the relationship so many times that it has become the norm. You start waiting for it to happen again. But there is good news. Restoration of trust can happen, but it will be up to the one who broke the trust to do the work to regain it back.

Regaining trust can be a very difficult process, but trust can be restored. It won't happen overnight. It may take months or even years. While we are going through the stage of trust restoration, we have to talk, and we have to come together and strengthen the trust bond that was broken. We have to put it all out there, lay all our cards on the table, no beating around the bush. We need to let our spouse know how they made us feel and exactly what it's going to take to make the relationship work.

We have to let our spouse know what we will and will not put up with in our relationship and what the consequences will be if they break the trust bond again. When we set consequences, we must stick to them. Because if we don't, nothing will ever change.

When we are trying to build our trust bond again, don't be afraid to seek professional help. Seek a good therapist or marriage counselor. It is important to rebuild the trust bond. If we never start to rebuild the foundation, the marriage won't withstand the storms of life.

Galatians 5:15-16 (NLT) states, "But if you are always biting and devouring one another, watch out! Beware of destroying one another."

Chapter 5

ROMANCE

&

INTIMACY

A Romantic Groove

Ramona Jones

"Have You Prayed Together Today?"

"There are three things that amaze me no, four things that I don't understand: how an eagle glides through the sky, how a snake slithers on a rock, how a ship navigates the ocean, how a man loves a woman" (Proverbs 30:18-19NLT).

Romance plays a very important part in marriage. It is a feeling of excitement and mystery associated with love.

My husband is a very romantic man. When we were first married, my husband would bring me flowers, write me poems, and our romantic dates would be eating a bucket of chicken sitting at the neighborhood park or the beach, sharing our dreams for the future. I remember he used to cut out the "Love Is" comic strips from the Daily Times newspaper and leave them on my pillow or in my car. (If you are not familiar with "Love Is" comic strips. Google it. They are the sweetest things ever.) As we grow older, he still buys me flowers and writes me poems. Our romantic dinners have moved to nice restaurants. But our favorite thing to do is still to have a bucket of chicken at the beach.

Romance is not just the man's responsibility. Ladies, we must bring some romance into the relationship as well. No, most men don't want flowers or love poems. But how about tickets to a game or cooking his favorite meal (even if it's not organic and healthy)? Touch him more. (Not sexually.) Put your hand on his knee, rub his arm while you talk, and my favorite, rub his head. (Take my word for it, ladies. If your man has had a tough day, rub his head, massage his neck, rub his temples… I'm tryna teach y'all something.)

And please, tell me of any man who wouldn't feel romanced to get "sex with a smile coupons" that he can redeem anytime he wanted. (Anytime.) Wait. Let me back up. I bet you're wondering why I said "sex with a smile" coupons instead of just sex coupons. Let me explain. When you gave him the gift you were trying to be romantic, right? Therefore, when it's time for him to redeem his coupon, you have to give him what the coupon says. Sex with a smile. And not that I'm not in the mood so come on over here and do your business so I can go to sleep kind of sex. Be romantic.

Being romantic doesn't take a lot of money. Take an evening walk through the neighborhood holding hands. Chill at home, turn off the lights, burn some candles, listen to some music, and sing some slow jams together. Give each other a massage or turn off all electronics and just talk about your dreams for the future, just because some of us may be a little older now, we still have dreams. Talk about them. (That's romance, ya'll.)

Romantic things are nice, and we all love them. But there also has to be intimacy in our marriage. Just in case you are not getting my meaning, when I say intimacy, I'm talking about sex. Making love, knocking boots, doing the do, hittin' it, tapping it, smashing whatever you choose to call it. It all comes down to that three-letter word *s-e-x*.

I once heard Pastor TD Jakes say, "Christians don't like to talk about sex." He said it's one of those things that Christians believe God turns his head and says go. People, it's OK to talk about sex. It's OK to have sex.

It's not that dirty, little, hidden secret that our parents of old made us believe. If you don't want to have sex with your spouse just as badly as they want to have it with you, then just like I said earlier, y'all doing something wrong. If you doing it wrong, take the time to make it right.

God created sex for husband and wife. He intended for it to be enjoyable. Sex between husband and wife is a beautiful thing. It's like a dance where sometimes he leads and sometimes she leads. Sex should flow like a sweet groove, a groove that is able to move from smooth jazz to hard rock and never miss a beat. (That's when you know y'all grooving to the same beat.)

Intimacy shouldn't start in the bedroom.

Touch each other. As I said in earlier chapters, I had to get used to my husband's affectionate side. This dude will kiss me, hug me, or grab my butt anywhere, even if I am standing in public. (He's been doing it for over thirty years. I've given up. He's never gonna stop.) Hold hands, hug, and kiss in public. Send a sexy text.

Know what you need and communicate.

The intimacy connection is different from any other connection you may share with your spouse. It brings you closer as a couple. We need to know what we need from our partners, and we need to communicate it.

If you have been in a relationship for years and you are not sexually satisfied, it's not your mate's fault. It's yours. If we are not getting what we need from our partner, it will weaken our marital bond. Teach your partner to satisfy you, and talk about what you need. It's imperative that we communicate our needs. If we don't communicate, this is when we start to believe we can get our needs met elsewhere and start allowing others to sneak into our intimacy bond. Don't be afraid or shy to be honest with your partner about what you need when it comes to intimacy. If you don't make them aware of what you need, don't be mad if you are not getting it. Now, you are bored with your sex life and sexually frustrated because you never made your spouse aware of what you needed.

Making love is an art.

Don't dip the brush in the paint and start making wild strokes. We must study our canvas, and get to know every part of it. Examine it from the top to the bottom and from the front to the back. Then, once we feel we know it, we need to be creative and use our imagination; we should take our time. When we begin to make strokes, we will create something beautiful, a masterpiece. Remember, we must practice our art continuously because practice makes perfect. The more we practice, the more of an expert we will become. But how can we practice without doing?

The answer to that question is we can't. We have to have sex. If there is nothing physically wrong with us, why are we not making love? It's impossible to have the deep intimacy that's needed to keep our marriages strong if we are only having sex on birthdays and anniversaries. Our intimacy bond will become weak or broken. We have to put forth an effort if we want to keep the bond strong. We invest our time into things that are important to us. It is worth the time, energy, and effort to build a satisfying sex groove.

Try your best not to always have tired sex.

I know this is difficult. We're tired. We've both worked all day. After we get home, the second part of our day begins. If we have children, we have to feed them, go over homework, talk about their day, make sure they bathe, and get them off to bed. Or we might be pet parents. We have to take our pet out for their evening potty walk and make sure they have food and fresh water. We finally get showered and lay down, just to think about all we have to do the next day. We want to make love we really do. So, we both agree to go ahead and do it, just so we can go to sleep. This is OK, sometimes. But that's not practicing the art of making love. That's just finger painting. Take a day off of work, and plan a romantic day together. Break up the routine. Go to a nice hotel and pamper yourselves. Avoid falling into the habit of tired sex. Relaxed and refreshed bodies are the cure for tired sex.

Stop making excuses for why you are not having sex with your spouse.

We have small kids, and they sleep with us. I'm just too tired. He likes to watch TV late, so most of the time, he sleeps on the couch or in his man cave. We work different schedules. I'm too old for all that. And the list goes on. If you have small children, put them down for the night early, or find someone to trade babysitting favors with. If you are tired, figure out why you are so tired all the time. Do you eat well? Are you exercising? Do you take vitamins or supplements? Do you need to visit your doctor? Yes, you may work different schedules. Decide to leave work early or take a sanity day. Some of us have a ton of vacation days just rolling over from one year to the next. Like I said before, take a day off, and set up a rendezvous at a nearby hotel. If you can't afford a hotel, rendezvous at home. If you have children, get them off to school, lock the door, close the curtains, and turn off the electronics. Light some candles and play some music. Ladies put on something sexy, and enjoy each other. I have a public service announcement for some of you. (You are not too old to have sex.) Healthy individuals can have sex well into their nineties. Figure it out, people.

Keep others out of your bedroom.

Don't bring others into your bedroom. (No, threesomes are not OK. I'm a pretty hospitable person. I'll share a meal with you, but I won't share my man.) You don't have to discuss with others everything you do in the privacy of your bedroom. That should be between you and your mate. My husband once said that if he wanted to wear a Batman suit and swing from the chandelier in our bedroom, that's his business. Well, that was OK with me. I'm sure I could find a Catwoman outfit for this dynamic duo. What? Eartha Kitt was still sexy when she was over eighty.

Keep it sexy.

Ladies, most men are visual. Add a little satin, silk, and lace to your bedroom attire. Guys, get a mani-pedi. A woman doesn't want callus, rough hands rubbing on her body. (Unless you're into that. To each his own.) But rough feet tearing up my sheets? Sorry, that ain't sexy.

Don't cheat.

I say again. Don't cheat. Don't cheat physically or emotionally. Yes, cheating emotionally is still cheating, and the bond can be damaged.

If you are not practicing the art of romance and intimacy, please start today. Start where you are. Send a text, card, or note. No one is asking you to write a sonnet. At least not yet. The effort that you invest will be appreciated. Never stop being romantic, and never stop making love. Practice, practice, practice, until you become the master of your art.

Chapter 6

COMMUNICATION

A Communication Groove

Darryl (DJ) Jones

'Have You Prayed Together Today?"

"Know this, my beloved brothers: let every person be quick to hear, slow to speak, slow to anger" (James 1:19 ESV).

Communication is the cornerstone of a great marriage. The ability to communicate is very important if it is your goal to build an exciting, nurturing, fun, and joyful marriage. We all enter a relationship with our own unique style of communication both verbal and non-verbal.

In our marriage, I am "The Talker." It is not uncommon to find me in deep conversation with an absolute stranger in the grocery store, restaurant, elevator, or anywhere I come in contact with people. Other people's experiences, perspectives, and points of view have always fascinated me.

In our marriage, one of the things that I love the most is our high communication I.Q. In the years that we have been married, we have developed the ability to communicate when things are going well and when we are experiencing challenges. At the base of communication, there must be a desire to understand the other person's point of view. It has been said that God gave us two ears and one mouth so that we can listen twice as much as we speak. In order for communication to take place in a marriage, there have to be two willing participants the speaker and the listener, a giver and a receiver.

In this aspect, communication is similar to making love. Now that I have your attention, let me tell you why I made that statement. When a man and woman make love, both can be pleased if there is a desire to please and receive pleasure. Both things take partners that are committed to each other and are willing to participate in pleasing each other. When I am listening to my wife, I make sure that I am looking at her and she has my full attention. There are few things more annoying than having someone look at the cell phone, computer, or TV when you are trying to have a serious conversation.

Everyone communicates differently. I will give you an

example. I manage a staff of six, and they are all ladies. I came home from work, and I told my wife that one of my employees broke up with her boyfriend and was crying. My wife asked me, "Is she OK; what happened?"

"I don't know."

She says, "What do you mean you don't know? Did you ask her any questions?"

"No, I did not. If she wanted me to know any additional information, she would have told me." My wife insisted that I should have asked her how she was feeling and if she was alright.

Now, my wife would have taken out a lamp and flashed it in her face and interrogated her! She would have known when they started dating, where they met, what caused the argument, what he said, and what she said until the actual breakup. Just kidding. My wife has the ability to get people to open up and pour their hearts out to her.

When I am talking with my wife, since I know how she communicates, I need to ask questions. This indicates to her that I am listening and engaged. If I am not asking questions, I need to give her the nonverbal signals like nodding my head or placing my hand on her leg or shoulder. This lets her know that I am connected.

My communication style is different from my wife's, and I process information differently than she does. If I tell her that something exciting happened at work today and I want to share it with her, she takes a seat and is ready to listen. I will say that I made a large sale today and closed a deal with a new client, and I am very excited about it. That is pretty much it. Just the facts and the numbers. Since she knows that this is the way that I communicate, she literally has to fight the urge to ask me detailed questions about what happened and how I felt during the process. However, if my wife wants to share something with me that happened at work, she is going to tell me every detail. What she said, what the other person said, what the weather was like, what she was wearing that day, what the other person was wearing, and how she was glad she wore her flats that day instead of heels.

Since I am a bottom-line kind of guy, I had to learn to communicate in a way that would be beneficial for my wife and me. It's a give and take, incorporating some of the things that she needs along with the things that I need to make sure we both are getting what we need in our communication.

Barriers to Communication.

What are some of the barriers that prevent us from being able to communicate with each other effectively? One of the main barriers is not listening. Now, understand what I am saying. You may hear someone, but are you actively listening? There are times when we are in such a hurry to get our point across that we are already thinking about our response before we have heard the other person's point of view. So, we must learn to be an active listener with an open mind so we can hear another point of view.

Another major barrier is when we are not open to another person's idea or perspective. This one can be major. When we are not open to an idea that is not our own, we put the other person in a defensive position. I have often said that I can disagree with you without being disagreeable. It really comes down to being open and willing to hear another person's perspective. Everyone has a point of view or idea. We must be willing to be open to others' ideas, as we would expect the same in return. It all comes down to how you present what you have to say.

It's not what you say, it's how you say it.

I remember when our children were young. When they wanted to do something that we as parents didn't disagree with, we would allow them to argue their case. Of course, this was my wife's idea. I was more of a because I said so kind of dad. But Ramona said, "Honey, let's hear what they have to say." I would agree, sometimes, to let them have their say. Every now and then, one of them would pop off in a way that I felt was disrespectful, as if they forgot who they were talking to. That's when I would have to shut the whole debate down and just say no. They would ask, "Dad, what did I say that was so bad?"

The answer would be, "It's not what you said, it's how you said it." My children may have thought they were making good points. And some of their points may have been considered if they had not said it in a way that I felt was unacceptable. We can't speak to our spouse any way and expect them to be OK with it. If our spouse points out to us that we spoke to them harshly, we don't get to tell them they are being sensitive, and this is the way I talk to everybody. They are not everybody; they are your spouse. Words hurt and the way you use them can cut deep.

For the most part, I am pretty mellow. I am never too high or too low. I'm pretty steady in my temperament. If I elevate my tone slightly, my wife asks me why I am yelling.

It is very important to watch our tone and the way we say things. I find it unnerving when I hear couples argue and begin to call each other names that are just way out of bounds. How do you recover from that? You can't just say, "I was upset, and I didn't mean it." Wouldn't it make more sense to not say damaging and hurtful words? Please don't tell me that it just slipped out. If you said it, you meant it. You wanted to hurt the person you say you love with your words.

This is a learned behavior, and it can be modified if you

want to change. There has to be a desire to build and strengthen your relationship. It is so easy to tear down and respond in anger. One of the things that Ramona and I have found to be very helpful when we are in a heated discussion is to pause. Either of us can say, "Can we discuss this later?" This way, we have a chance to gather our thoughts instead of exploding in a fit of anger and saying things that are hurtful and damaging.

Listen. Repeat to make sure you understand.

When I forget something my wife told me, I always joke with her and say, "You know I don't listen to you when you talk." I don't know how many fights can be avoided or how many marriages can be saved if we listen. It's easy for us to say I'm listening to you. But the truth of the matter is, it really depends on the subject matter if someone wants to listen. If my wife is talking to me about something that pertains to her health, I'm 100% ears. If it's about our grandchildren, I'm about 98% in. If it's about our adult kids, I'm about 90% in. If she starts talking to me about the budget and paying bills, I go in and out with listening. That's only because I know that the money is there for the bills, and we decided over thirty years ago that she was better at handling paying bills than me. I'm just like every other guy, sometimes I just half listen. And just like every other guy, we pay for it later.

Listening is very crucial for a relationship. Not only are we listening for the day to day things, but we also have to listen so we can hear our spouse's wants and needs. Can you imagine your spouse coming to you one day and saying I want a divorce? And you ask why. They say you never gave them any of their wants or needs. And you say they never told you. And they say no, you never listened.

Too many directions or topics. Stay on Point. Bottom line It:

Of course, this is my favorite communication characteristic. My wife had to learn this about me. I'm a bottom-line guy. If I could wear a t-shirt every day with an arrow pointing down and line under it, I would. Bottom line it. Give me the bottom line. I don't need a whole soliloquy of the how, what, when, where, and why. Just bottom line it. Don't set me up to fail. Don't make me go around the corner just to tell me what you needed me to do was something right here at the house. I don't need too many directions; just tell me what you need from me. As close as I am to my wife after thirty-five years of marriage, I still have to tell her from time to time, I am not a mind reader. Just tell me what you want.

When our youngest son was a teenager, my wife would say, "James, take out the trash, clean your room, and oh, by the way, take the truck, have it washed, put gas in it, and run to the store and pick up this, that, and the other." I would have to constantly tell her she was setting him up to fail. She gave him too many directions. He is bound to forget something. I know I might get a lot of flak for this one, but I'm going to say it, anyway. Women are the worst offenders of too many topics at one time. What are you talking about? What do you want? What do you need? Just tell us, plain and simple what it is you want. It drives me crazy when I hear women say, "He should know what is wrong with me; he should know what I want. He should know why I am not happy."

We admit it women. We can't figure it out. We don't know what you want. We don't know what you need. We don't know what's wrong with you. We're not that smart. Don't set us up to fail. For the sake of all that is good. Please, just tell us. We don't want to play twenty questions or guess. Just tell us. Get to the point. Bottom line it. I promise you, it will add years to both our lives and our marriages.

Just listen don't try to fix it.

I'm a protector when it comes to my family, so this one was a hard one for me. When there is a challenge or problem, my analytical side kicks in. If there is a problem, I think it through and come up with options or solutions. This is just the way my mind works.

When my wife communicates to me that something is bothering or hurting her, my first response is to get into protective mode. I want to address and fix anything that might be causing her hurt or harm. I found out over the years that she does not need me to step in on everything. Although my wife is a lady, she still got a little hood in her, and she can handle a lot of her own battles. And most of her problems she didn't need me to fix, she just needed to vent. Guys, we have to learn to just listen and not always want to fix her problems. It's OK to ask her if she needs you to handle it or if she just needed to talk about it.

I am not telling you that I learned how to do this overnight. It was a process. Now, I can tell when she wants to vent or if it's something she needs me to get involved in. It all came from listening to her. You will get bonus points if you don't interrupt her when she is venting. When my wife vents, it gives me mental anxiety, (smile) only because her creative brain works differently than my analytical brain. She starts in the middle, goes to the end, and back to the beginning, just like she writes sometimes. However, I have learned how to let her vent and not interrupt. I believe she appreciates it.

Watch your body language.

My wife has been blessed with the gift of discernment. She is not much of a talker, but she listens and watches people. She has an ability to read people's body language. She has saved me from doing business with people who down the line showed their bad business practices.

We have to pay attention to our partner's body language. Are they folding their arms when you are speaking or tapping their feet like they are bored with what you are saying? Maybe they are narrowing and rolling their eyes as if they are not interested.

What does your body language say when your wife or husband is speaking to you? Are you engaged and actively listening? My wife does something that I think is really an excellent idea. When we are watching a program on TV and I say to her, "I want to tell you something," she grabs the remote and pauses the program and says, "What's on your mind, honey?" Right there she is teaching me how she wants me to respond to her when she needs to talk to me. We can learn so much from each other, but we have to watch, listen, and learn from each other and be prepared to act. She modeled the type of response that she needs from me.

Remove all distractions.

This one right here is still hard for me because I am a creature of habit and a multitasker. When I get home from work, I bring my phone and my iPad into the living room where my wife and I watch TV. Although I know I can listen to my wife, watch whatever chick power movie she chose to watch, catch the score of the game, and return a couple of work emails, all at the same time, when she wants to talk, I know I have to remove my distractions. Men, we need to pay attention to what we are saying yes to. Man, I really hope some guys are reading this book. If I weren't distracted and was paying attention when Ramona asked, I would not have gotten suckered into writing these chapters.

Throughout our marriage journey, we should learn to communicate in effective ways. In ways where we can be open, honest, and vulnerable. The way we communicate with our spouse will make the difference between a strong or weak union. I don't believe that anyone has all the answers. What works for my marriage might not work for yours. My goal is to give you some food for thought and suggestions so you can find a way to communicate that is meaningful and will work for your marriage. Sometimes, when we read about someone else's experience, it will cause us to think about methods and ideas that would be beneficial to our relationship. Remember, marriage is a groove a smooth love song. The melody, the pace, the tempo, everything works and flows smoothly together. If in the middle of the song, the pace changes and the melody is not matching the groove, something is off. Your communication has lost its rhythmic flow.

Chapter 7

CHILD REARING

A Family Groove

Ramona Jones

'Have You Prayed Together Today?"

"Behold, children are a heritage from
the Lord,
the fruit of the womb a reward" (Psalm
127:3 ESV).

The decision to have children can be a most exciting time for most married couples. You are having a little you or him. But sometimes, having a child is not exciting at all. This can be for a number of reasons. There are those who never wanted children at all. (Make sure your mate knows this. Don't get married and let them find out after years of being married to you that you never wanted children. That's very selfish.)

Then, there are the planners. You have your five-year plan all mapped out. You are going to graduate college, land a great job, move up the corporate ladder, and have people reporting to you before you're thirty. You'll have your bank account tight and own your first piece of property. Then, and only then, will you have children. Sounds great, right? Even the most well laid out plan can take a major detour. One night of getting caught up in the moment, and now, you have entered into the Twilight Zone otherwise known as parenthood. Once we make the decision to bring a life into this world, that little person is our responsibility; they are depending on us. We are to love, guide, teach, and protect them.

There are millions of books that teach us how to rear children. They teach us how to communicate, how to broach different topics with them, and the best way to deal with children with special needs. Rearing children is a lot of work in and of itself. But being the parent of a special needs' child can be double the work.

It is important for us, the parents, to take a time-out. That's right. I said it. We, the parents, need a time-out. We need to take time away from our children. We need time when we are not hearing mommy or daddy unless, of course, your boo is referring to you that way.

Couples, if you don't take a time-out from your children, they will weary you. This includes both young children and adult children. Yes, yes, and again, I say yes. Yes, our children sometimes make us weary, pissed off, tired, mad, and stressed. But just because our children are stressing us out and driving us crazy, they are still our children. It is still our responsibility to rear the children we decided to have.

Whether you have children together or enter into a relationship with someone who has children, parenting and rearing children is work. Children can cause a lot of joy in our marriages, and they can cause a lot of conflict.

Blending Families

Stepping into a ready-made family can prove to be difficult sometimes. I know Jada Pinkett-Smith has everyone saying, these are our bonus children, but some of these children can become very unruly when their parents start new relationships. Children sometimes resent the new spouse because they think that if you weren't with their mom or dad, that their parents may get back together. Darryl and I were somewhat of a blended family. I had a daughter when we married; we share one daughter together, and we took custody of our two nephews when one was nine years old and the other six months old.

I know that most blended families come from spouses having children before they become a union, but we are all still just blending together to make a family. When we decide to marry and there are children involved that are not our own, we need to make sure we know our role in the life of that child.

We can't just jump into the relationship with the child as if we are their biological parent and start being a dictator. Get to know the child, and get to know the child's actual parent. If at all possible, all parents should discuss together what rules you have for the child or children, when they are in your home. We must all understand that there are rules in each marriage and family. You may not like the word rules, but that's exactly what it comes down to.

John 14:6 (NIV) says, Jesus said to him, I am the way, and the truth, and the life. No one comes to the Father except through me. It's a rule. You can't come to the Father unless you go through the Son. God has rules for us to follow in order for us to be in relationship with Him. So, why shouldn't we have rules to be in a relationship with each other?

In a marriage, you both should set and know what the rules of your household are. We must know what works for our marriage and family and not what works for the Jones's, no pun intended. It's all trial and error. Don't expect to get the rules right the first time. And you also have to periodically adjust the rules. Try different things. If it works, stick with it. If it doesn't, make another adjustment.

Consider this, regardless of the adjustments you may try to make for children. Some children may just straight out not like you, no matter how hard you try. We must try to be patient with children. Remember, they are just children; they will continue to try you until something is said and rules are put in place. If bad behavior is not addressed, children will take advantage of you and cause conflict between you and your spouse.

Remember that there are several different attitudes and personalities under one roof. You and your spouse should always have a united front when it comes to your children. Once they see a weak link, they will attack that link until they break it. Never allow your children to see you treat each other badly. When children see their parents disrespect each other or treat each other badly, they feel it's OK for them to treat you in that same manner. This causes a lot of conflict in the home.

When I got married, I treated my husband with respect in front of my daughter at all times. When I had an issue with something, he said to her, we would discuss it behind closed doors. I never let her hear me disagree with any of his punishments because children are smart. They will use that to cause problems between you and your spouse. Just as long as the punishments are not abusive, stick to it and give the child a little grace later, after the two of you have discussed the matter in private.

A young lady once told me that she and her husband would argue in front of their children so the children would know that mommy and daddy have misunderstandings and are not perfect. She said they should know that everyone argues. I didn't agree with that. I don't think that children should have to be burdened with adult issues. They are children. Let them live the fantasy for a while.

Pour positivity into your children.

When we bring these little people into the world, we should love them, protect them, and teach them. We want them to grow up to be respectable, responsible, and capable adults. It is important that we start building our children's character and self-esteem early. Tell your daughter she is beautiful and she's smart. Make sure she is comfortable in her own skin. Make sure she loves the body, the face, the hair, and the skin color that God gave her. Tell your son he's handsome and he's smart. Make sure he loves the body, the face, the hair, and the skin color that God gave him. It's OK to enhance our beauty, but first, we have to accept our own natural beauty.

Accept their differences.

We raised four children with four different personalities. We, as parents, must understand that each of our children is different. (This is very important, so listen to me closely.) We can't expect that just because our children are siblings or that they grew up in the same household, they should all act alike, think alike, be on the same intellectual level, or have the same level of creativity. Some children are more affectionate than others. Does that mean you should only hug and spend time with the one who shows you the most affection? Of course not. Continue to show affection to the child who is not as affectionate. We have to kiss and hug them, spend one-on-one time with them, even if they act as if they don't want to spend time with us. And just because one of your children gets straight *A's* without a struggle doesn't mean that the other children should be able to master work just as easy. They are all different.

We also have to watch what we speak over our children. We shouldn't say she's going to be the fast one, or he's the dumb one, that's the sneaky one, or that's the one who doesn't like affection. I remember when I was a child, people would always say I was mean. I guess I looked mean. I was never really mean. But after hearing it for years, I started to believe it, so I started to act mean. Remember, if you hear something long enough, you start to believe it. So, be careful what you speak over your children. They will turn out to be what you programmed in their minds.

Discipline.

When rearing children, we can't have just one set standard of discipline to deal with all of our children. What works on one child may not work on the other. My husband and I raised two boys and two girls. Most of the time we could just talk to our children and they would straighten up. But there were times where we had to hand out punishments. We also didn't spare the rod. (It was a different time.)

As a couple, we must come together and decide effective ways to discipline our children with love. But we need to be persistent in letting our children know that there are consequences when they choose to act up. Discipline is very important when rearing children. Wait, I think I need to say that again. Discipline is very important when rearing children. Discipline helps the child to develop an understanding of right and wrong behavior throughout their lives.

Children learn by example, so it is important for us to have a positive approach when guiding your children into adulthood. Have you ever witnessed an adult have a full-blown tantrum? You think to yourself, *Oh, wow. Are they going to fall on the floor and start kicking and screaming or hold their breath until they get their way?* Those are examples of adults who have had no discipline or proper guidance as children. There has to be some type of discipline or our children will not understand right from wrong. If they don't understand right from wrong, it's probably because there were never any consequences for bad behavior while they were growing up.

It is our responsibility as parents to teach our children how to control their emotions when they are in difficult situations. My daughter tells me that my grandson gets mad and starts to cry if the teachers don't call on him. He knows the answers and wants to answer all the questions. She has to explain to him that there are several children in the class, and the teacher has to give others an opportunity to answer the questions, as well. So, when it's not your turn, you have to wait without getting angry. He doesn't like it, but he understands he has to control himself.

We have to teach our children how to have self-discipline and respect for others. We must teach them effective ways to solve problems and teach them how to be independent and how to interact with others. In today's society, spanking and yelling are not the acceptable way of disciplining and that's OK. When Darryl and I see our children discipline our grandchildren, it makes me think that sometimes the time-out method works better than a spanking. (If not for them, for me. I don't like it when my grands get spankings.) However, some form of discipline is always needed when rearing children. Because let's keep it real, when our children get in public acting out, the first thing you will hear is, where is the mother.

Religious Beliefs.

My husband grew up in church as a PK (Preachers Kid). He often says that when he was a child, if he weren't at church, he was at Kaiser because something had better have been wrong with him in order for him to miss church. As a child, his family spent a lot of time at church. Sunday School, morning worship, YPWW (Young People, Willing Workers), and then evening worship all on Sundays. Then, there was choir rehearsal on Tuesdays, Bible study on Wednesday, and Purity Classes on Friday. And almost all of his friends were church kids as well.

Growing up for me was a little different. I went to church sometimes, but it was not a mandatory thing in our home. I grew up with a single mother who was rearing four children. She worked a lot, so we had a little bit more freedom. I think my older sisters went to church more than I did when we were younger.

Aretha Franklin song Son of a preacher man said; *The only one who could ever reach me was the son of a preacher man.* Guess what? I married the preacher's son, y'all. For most church girls, their sole desire is to be a part of the pastor's family. For me, not so much. But check this out, not only did I marry the pastor's son, but I'm also married to a minister. Who would have ever thought it? He tricked me, y'all. When we married, he was the prodigal son before he came to himself. (Read Luke chapter 15.)

He was my party dude and my drinking buddy who one day came to me and told me that the Lord was calling him back. You've heard of the saying a wolf in sheep's clothing. My husband was the opposite he was a sheep in wolf's clothing. Imagine my surprise. The Lord is calling you back? Calling you back where? And am I supposed to go with you? I tell you, we went through the storms and rains but we made it.

We had a rocky year after he did his 180 degree turn from bad boy back to church boy. And I didn't think we were going to make it. But as the scripture says, with love and kindness have I drawn thee (Jeremiah 31:3).

If you are a religious person, it might be important to you to raise your children with the same beliefs that you have. I don't subscribe to just letting your children decide. It's our job to spiritually guide and direct our children. The devil is busy taking control of them. He is taking control of them because we, as parents, have not introduced them to Jesus and given them the solid foundation. We are letting our children decide who they worship, and because we are letting them make their own spiritual decisions, we have way too many young people saying they don't believe in God.

You may not agree with me, but I believe our young people are choosing to believe in other gods because the presentation to the one and only God is not appealing. He is not appealing to them because when we introduce them to Christ, the first thing we do is give our young people a list of one hundred things they cannot do. So, before they can even develop the relationship with God, they give up. They give up because we are making God seem like he's unreachable. Nobody wants to be a part of something that's unattainable. God's love is not unreachable. God loves us. Romans 5:8 (KJV) says, "But God commendeth his love toward us, in that, while we were yet sinners, Christ died for us."

Instead of being a dictator, we need to discuss our spiritual beliefs with our children. Explain to them why we do things a certain way and answer any questions they may have. When our children were still at home, we would have Bible study at home. We would have them read scriptures with us and answer questions if they had any.

We, as parents, have to remember that we no longer live in a "because I said so" generation. Young people have questions and need answers. I find that when people can't explain why they do things a certain way, they may not understand themselves. They just know that we do it this way because this is the way it's always been done. This reminds me of a story I once read. And I'm sure you heard it or some version of it before.

A newly wedded couple was cooking dinner together for all the bride's family. The new husband watched his new wife prepare a ham. She removed the outer wrap, cut off the end of the ham, and then threw the end of the ham into the trash under the sink.

"Why'd you do that?" asked the husband.

"It's how my mother has always done it," the new bride replied.

"Why'd your mother do it?" asked the husband.

"I don't know," said the wife.

"Could you ask her?" said the husband.

"Sure," replied his wife.

The bride went to her mother and asked, "Mother, when you cook a ham, why do you cut off the end and throw it away?"

"It's the way your grandmother always did it. You'll need to ask her," said the mother. So, the bride went to her grandmother with the same question.

"Sweet child." The grandmother laughed. "I cut off the end of the ham because the ham was always too big to fit into the only small pot we had!"

Isn't that just funny? But we approach religion the same way. We have beliefs or traditions that we pass down from generation to generation, and we really don't understand why we believe this way, or why we do things a certain way. All we know is this is the way we've always done it.

People will twist and misinterpret scriptures to make them fit their own way of teaching or their way of living and thinking. It is important to teach and encourage our children to read the Bible and get an understanding for themselves, and not just believe what another person's interpretation is.

And we surely don't want them doing it because this is the way we've always done it. We want to lead our children into a loving relationship with God so that they will always have a solid foundation. In our home, we live by Proverbs 22:6 (KJV). "Train up a child in the way he should go: and when he is old, he will not depart from it." We have to train our children on a solid foundation. When things get hard in their lives and troubled times come, and they will come, they need to know who to call on.

When I first came to the Lord after a year of fighting against it, I had a lot of questions about the way things were done in church. I have never been the go along to get along kind of girl. I'm sure I stressed out a lot of Pastors, Sunday school teachers, Bible study teachers, and Pastor's wives. Sorry, but things have to make sense to me. I don't mind following, but I have to know where I'm going. I had to study and understand for myself. We can't just listen to someone teach on a certain subject, but never read it for ourselves. We will take someone else's interpretation, and that's all we know. We shouldn't be afraid to ask questions and expect answers that make sense. Not just because this is the way we've always done it. I love Sunday school and Bible study. I like to ask questions to spark conversation. It's not that I don't have an answer or know the answer to my questions, I like to hear others opinions.

2 Timothy 2:15 (KJV) says, "Study to shew thyself approved unto God, a workman that needeth not to be ashamed, rightly dividing the word of truth."

Education.

Let's talk about our children and education. When we choose to move to a certain area, we must consider if the home fits our family, if the neighborhood is safe, and if the school system is a good one for our children. When it comes to education, we must make sure our children are getting the best education we can make available. Education for our children is not only for academic learning but also to learn how to interact with their peers and with authority figures. It is important that we follow up with our children regularly. Ask them about what's going on at school. Don't just ask how was school today. And allow them to say, "It was good." Conversation ended.

Ask open-ended questions. Children have a lot going on in their lives. Some things we may not ever think should be going on in our children's lives are happening. Don't think because your child is in elementary school that you don't have to worry. Children as young as seven or eight want to know about things that we would never think children their age would be thinking about. Sex, drugs, homosexuality, sex change, suicide, gender assignment, same-parent households, and the list goes on.

Check your children's phones and computers. We need to see what sites our children have access to. Parents need to know if our children are using those expensive electronic devices for study purposes and not just for posting selfies, Snapchat, Instagram, and sites that I've never even heard of before. We need to know if our children are being cyber-bullied or being romanced by some weirdo or thinking about shooting up the school or joining a suicide challenge, or they are so depressed, and have been researching ways to commit suicide.

The new thing I've been hearing about is cybersex. Young people are vividly articulating what they are doing to each other sexually online but have never touched, and some have never met. Our children are very savvy with electronics, so try to stay as computer literate as possible.

Parents, check your younger children's backpacks. You would be amazed at what you might find. The assignments they forget to turn in, the homework they forgot they had, the notes that the teacher sent home to you a week ago. And let's not forget my favorite, the infamous "Oh my god, picture day is tomorrow."

With your older children, make sure they attend school every day. Call the school and speak with the attendance secretary. Ask your children daily about their homework. Ask to see it and discuss what they learned. I know sometimes we feel like we don't have time for all that. But we need to make time. Be involved parents. I remember my husband would do surprise visits to our children's schools. Even our children's friends would run to class when they saw him show up on campus. Word would get to our children that Papa Jones was on campus.

We formed relationships with our children's teachers and counselors, and each of them had all of our contact information. They had no problem calling if our children misbehaved.

Make appointments with your child's counselor to make sure they are on track in school. I would never want to find out that my child couldn't graduate because their credits were short and I didn't know. We have to try and stay on top of what our children are doing.

Watch and Pray.

Matthew 26:41 starts off by saying watch and pray. I know prayer changes things, but we can't just pray; we also have to watch. We need to pay attention to our children, their attitude, personality, and behavior. Don't just write it off as a child or teenager with an attitude for no reason. Children have so many things they are dealing with that we may have never dealt with.

With all of the electronics we afford our children, they can be bullied on these devices. They can read about how a young person thought that committing suicide was the answer to their problems. They can see children being allowed to live as one sex when they were born another. They can get involved in strange religions. Some say this is just how it is. I say, it's time to take action. We have to do just what Matthew 26:41 says. Watch and Pray.

There are so many depressed young people. They think they are weird and nobody likes them. They have low self-esteem. They think they are ugly, fat, skinny, too dark, too light, dumb, or too smart. It is important for us to prepare them as much as we can for life's pitfalls.

Let's face it, kids are mean. They were mean when I was young, and they are going to continue to be mean. Some of the kids today don't have tough skin. Some have never had a fight. Not having friends when you are young is tough. They think everyone can make friends except them. So, they think the only way to escape their sad, lonely, or misfit feeling is ending their lives. I have never witnessed so many stressed young people. When I was a kid, the only thing I was worried about was if I looked cute in the outfit I chose to wear that day and making it home before the streetlights came on. Now, kids are stressed out because of what's going on in their friend's household and stressed about mom and dad's business. They are stressed wondering if they are ever going to make a friend.

When I was a child, I knew my mom had hard times raising four children as a single parent, but she didn't make it my business as to how she was handling her household bills and business. All I knew is we ate meals every day, we had clothes to wear, and we lived inside. Parents, stop discussing your business in front of your children. They are listening, even when you think they aren't. There is no way a child can sit in the room with adults who are talking and just look at TV. They are listening to every word you are saying. That movie they are pretending to watch is not that interesting, and it's a repeat anyway. Don't have your child depressed over things that shouldn't concern them.

We have to teach our children to love the Lord, love their own company, love and respect themselves, and others. And to not let others define who they are. (Remember, it's hard to teach what you haven't learned yourself.)

The Bond.

It is very important that we form a bond with our children. We were fortunate that we were able to sit at the table every night with our children and have dinner. We would talk as a family. I am not saying that by us having dinner with our children daily that they always told us everything that was going on in their lives because, as we all know, that didn't happen. But we formed a bond with our children where they could communicate with us. To this day, the bond that we forged with our children still exists. I communicate with both my daughters almost every day. Either they call me, or we have a mother-daughter messenger conversation. I talk to my son at least once a week.

When our children were young, we watched TV together and played board games and video games. When we visit our adult children's homes or they visit ours, we still like to eat meals and watch TV together. My son still wants to challenge his dad in Monopoly.

While hanging out with our children, we began to learn the differences in each one. You will find that some of our children are outspoken, some are shy, some learn easy, some may take a little longer to learn things, some are upfront, and some are sneaky. We should learn how to deal with and accept the individuality of each child. As the mother of four, I tried not to let too much get by me in our home. I had some sneaky children in my group. (But as the old saying goes, you can't out play a player.) I did room checks. I would check through drawers, under mattresses, closets, and their computers not really looking for anything in particular, but making sure nothing got past me.

You may say that this was an invasion of my children's privacy. I say you have no privacy until your name is on the rent or mortgage agreement. Privacy is how bombs are made and babies are conceived under your roof. I had no desire to visit my child in prison or to raise a baby that my baby made.

When it came to my husband and the children, he could be the gentle giant, or he could become the roaring bear. I hated when the bear got poked. I spent a lot of time smoothing the path when the children had something major to ask him especially when it came to our daughters. This dude had such an old school double standard he would make me so angry. Sometimes I wanted to chop him up in bite-size pieces (inside joke).

But we learned to compromise. Just like I had to learn to let down my defensive wall, he had to learn how to compromise on child-rearing. Sometimes, the rod is not the answer. I had to help Darryl understand that a talk, just listening, or a hug, might work just as affectively.

Being a parent is not an easy job. Some parents think if they are their children's friend, they will have a better relationship. I once had a teacher tell me that I should be my oldest daughter's best friend. She was ten at the time. I didn't subscribe to that theory. That may work for some, but my children didn't need me to be their bestie, they needed me to be their mom. Now that they are adults, I can be friends with my children because I am no longer responsible for rearing them.

We must do our best when rearing our children. It's our job as their parents to protect them. If you have children and you are dating, don't allow every man or woman to be alone with your children. Don't get so caught up in the relationship that you are not paying attention to the children. If you are going to become a blended family, take notice of how the other children are treating your children. Remember, adults are not the only ones who assault and abuse children. Children assault and abuse other children physically, mentally, and sexually.

As your children become adults, they will let you know how well you did as a parent. They will either tell you verbally that you sucked as a parent or they will show you. (Have you ever heard the saying I can show you better than I can tell you?) If your children don't really like to be around you when they become adults or they do the forced awkward visits just because it's your birthday, Mother's or Father's Day, you have your answer. There was a bond broken somewhere along the way. The good news is those bonds can be rebuilt. You must understand that in order to rebuild broken bonds with your children there may be some apologies or explanations that need to take place. After that has taken place, some will be totally mended, some bonds will be hanging together by one thread, and some will never be restored.

Parents with adult children.

It's OK for us to help our adult children with our grandchildren. But at some point, we need to be finished rearing children and focus on ourselves. My husband and I see our grandchildren often. We love our little crew of six grands. We visit, we face-time, and we help with their needs and some of their wants, and support most of their activities. But we don't want to raise them. (Yes, I said it) Some grandparents may want to raise their grandchildren, and some have to raise their grandchildren. I pray God gives those grandparents double blessings. Call us selfish, we're ok with that. We reared four children who became self-sufficient adults. No. We didn't miss anything while rearing our children. And no. We don't feel a need to start over.

We also need to understand that we can no longer dictate the way our children choose to live their lives. They are adults now. We can't choose where they live, where they work, who their friends are, who they date, or who they marry. I have seen parents not go to their child's wedding because they didn't approve of who they were marrying. Sorry, but I'm not going to ruin my relationship with my child because of who they choose to marry; they will always be my baby. I may not like the choices they make, but I will be there to support them.

We also can't choose whether they choose to attend church.

If the seed was planted a long time ago when they were young, you did your job. They already know right from wrong; why are you stressing yourself out trying to raise a grown person?

I realize it's hard sometimes. Especially when you see them taking the wrong path or getting involved with the wrong person. But we have to allow our adult children room to grow and learn from their own mistakes. If we raised them well, then we must trust that they were actually listening. There is nothing more rewarding than when you hear your adult child repeat something that you taught them, and say to you "Mom, Dad, I was listening."

Rearing children is hard work, but if we do our job and do it well, when our babies become adults you can then say we did our job. And job well done.

Chapter 8

Unrealistic Expectations

A Realistic Groove

Darryl (DJ) Jones

"Have You Prayed Together Today?"

"Now unto him that is able to do exceeding abundantly above all that we ask or think, according to the power that worketh in us . . ." (Ephesians 3:20 KJV).

I was very fortunate to see an excellent example of marriage growing up. My parents have been married for over sixty years. It is not just about the longevity of their marriage, even though that in and of itself is impressive. The thing that has stood out to me is that I have never heard my father raise his voice to my mother above his normal speaking voice. This impacted me in a very significant way. I always wanted to be married. I believe I was around five when I first said I wanted a wife. I wanted to be married, and I wanted to have a relationship built on love, honor, and respect. To see this modeled by my parents helped lay the foundation for what I wanted in my marriage. My wife is a multi-talented, phenomenal woman. She has been saying for years that she was going to write a book on the subject of marriage. Now, how she got me to take part in writing this book with her, I will never know. (What you won't do for love as the song goes.)

***From Ramona**. (The truth is, I was rubbing his head when I asked. Remember what I told y'all in the intimacy chapter about rubbing his head.)

She's trying to get me back for jumping into her chapters. As I was saying, being married to a writer is very interesting, to say the least. In mid-conversation, my wife will ask me to repeat something I said. This means it was a thought or foundation for something that she wants to write about. Watching her creative process is really quite interesting. It is a completely different experience getting involved and participating in writing with her.

My wife and I are from two different backgrounds. Our upbringing could not be any more different. Each one of us brings something unique to our marriage. I have learned a great deal from her, and I am sure that she has learned some things from me as well. Our children tell us that we are corny. That is fine with us. It's great to have someone that gets my jokes. And she laughs at them, too! Many people will say that we are "old school" in the way we treat each other. I will say that what we do works for us.

It is important that we know what we need from our marriages and also know what our expectations for our marriage are, keeping in mind a lot of people have unrealistic expectations. Having these unrealistic expectations sometimes makes us miss out on the person that God has for us. So, let me start by saying throw away those lists! Hear me out. Some of us want to be married but have a list of all the requirements that a person must have to be our potential mate. I'm going to start with some of the things that I have heard women say are on their list. They are in no particular order.

Will talk when the need arises versus trying to put it off until later.

Come on now, ladies. Sometimes, it's best if you allow us to put it off until later. I'm just keeping it real. Sometimes, what a man will say to you when you feel the need has arisen for the two of you to talk versus what we might have said if you would have let us put it off until we are really ready to talk, may be the very thing that saved our marriage. But hey, y'all want to say just one of those days, don't take it personal when y'all turn into what my wife refers to as Sybil. Well, don't take it personal when we turn into the Hulk.

He will not watch ESPN endlessly, and he will not judge me for watching rachet TV.

I agree with this one fellas. We don't need to watch ESPN endlessly. We also need to mix in A&E and, my favorite, the Discovery Channel. I write this laughing because my wife is forever talking smack about my Discovery Channel shows, but she knows all the characters and is always asking questions about what's going on when the episodes are on. But seriously, fellas, sometimes we have to watch a show that she likes, even if it is what I consider rachet TV. Are those shows that she thinks would be a good show for the two of you to watch together?

Guys, you know the shows I'm talking about. Those shows that you would have never, ever, ever chosen if you were watching TV by yourself. My wife often ropes me into TV series. I start watching them with her, then, after a season or two, she gets bored with them. Well, I'm all in. Now, I have to know if Tamar is still mad at her sisters or if the handmaids are ever going to get from "under his eye." And who killed Ghost? I have to see how it ends.

He will want to spend every waking second with you.

Man, when I saw this one, it gave me pause. Who has time for this? As much as I love my wife and love spending quality time with her, neither I nor my wife would want to spend every waking second with each other. We work daily. I like to walk or ride my bike by myself; it gives me time to clear my head and think. My wife likes to take a chair, her favorite hat, and her computer and sit by the water at the beach by herself and write. We don't need to spend that much time together. (My wife corrected me; she said, "It doesn't say that you are going to spend every waking second together. It says you want to.")

I looked at her and said, "I don't want to." All she could do was laugh. Because she doesn't want to spend every waking moment with me either.

Will call and not text.

Sometimes, all we have time to do is text you, especially if we are at work. I make it a point to call my wife at least once per day. All other communication is done via email or text. I'm busy and she's busy; if I don't need an immediate response, I can wait for a response to an email or text. In the time we live in, people really don't talk on the phone anyway; they prefer an electronic message. Don't be mad he's still communicating with you.

He will be tall.

Because I am a tall man, I hear a lot of ladies saying that they want a tall husband. My wife loves the fact that I'm tall as well. When she wears heels, she never has to worry about being taller than me. But when it comes time to shop for me and she sees the prices I have to pay to dress this tall body, she shudders. Ladies, all men are not tall. Some of you are barely five feet, anyway. What's wrong with an average height man? His height is not what makes him a man.

He will be good-looking.

Who is the judge of who looks good and who doesn't? Maybe you should just say good-looking to you. Regardless of how he looks to others, if he is good-looking to you, that's all that matters.

He must earn six figures or more.

What if he has the potential to eventually earn six figures? Or what if he doesn't earn a six-figure income, but he's a hardworking man who handles his business and loves and takes care of his family? And while I'm at it, do you earn six figures?

He must be able to buy me a ring that is two carats or more.

When I hear women make this comment, they come off as materialistic. Are you marrying the man, or do you just want to show off your piece of jewelry? Women will actually go out and buy their own ring or go with the man to choose it. I'm an old school guy; I believe the man should be allowed to choose the ring. We can buy you other jewelry that you can choose. Allow him to choose your ring. This particular ring is from the heart. If he can afford two carats and that is what he chooses to present you with, that's fine. However, if he can't afford to give you a ring of that size, will you choose not to marry him?

He must have a sense of humor.

In marriage, you need a sense of humor; you can't take life so seriously. It's so important that you laugh together as a couple. I said before my wife laughs at my jokes. I know my jokes are corny. I'm a corny dude, and she digs that. One of my many nicknames for my wife is twisty. She can take an old saying that has been said the same way for years and twist it up with another old saying and make it sound like it was supposed to be said that way. It just cracks me up because sometimes they sound better the way she says them. We should laugh with each other and at each other; it's OK.

He must love God.

Some of y'all need to be more specific when you say… " love God." What is the prerequisite of the way he has to love God? Does he have to love God the same way you love God? What if he has a personal relationship with God, prays, fasts, and has great faith? What if instead of him giving to the church all the time, he helps a single mom buy groceries or helps a college student buy books? What if he helps a couple catch up on their bills? As long as he has a committed relationship with God and is in regular fellowship at Church with other believers, isn't that what matters?

I just named a few things on the list women create, but my first question would be, "Do you want a husband, or are you training someone for the 'Love me like I tell you Olympics?'" I am not saying that you should not have an idea of some of the characteristics and qualities that you desire in a husband. Just don't have unrealistic expectations. Granted, there are some things that are deal breakers. I would suggest focusing on the positive.

Take a look at this scripture. (Yes, I am unashamedly Christian, and the Bible serves as my guide to life and my decision making.)

Genesis 2:24 (KJV) says, "Therefore shall a man leave his father and his mother, and shall cleave unto his wife: and they shall be one flesh."

Based on this scripture, I would say there are four basic qualifications that a man should have in order to be considered marriage material.

1. Man. One that honors God and puts God first.

2. Leave. Get out of your parents' home, sibling's home, homeboys' home, and prepare for a wife.

3. Cleave. To adhere closely, to stick to.

4. One Flesh. Spiritual and physical union.

When a man has these four qualities, then it becomes a matter of if the two of you are compatible. Are you both attracted to each other? Do you share similar values on faith, family, and finances?

Now, let's get to the man's list; this one will be a little easier for me because when I was younger, I had a list.

She must be physically attractive.

This was at the top of my list. She had to look good. Sorry, but I can see what you look like first before I can see your personality. Make sure she is physically attractive to you. I know some of the women are reading this and saying everyone is beautiful, blah, blah, blah. And I agree. But every woman is not physically attractive to me. And I'll say the same thing I said above. She just has to be physically attractive to you. I may look at her and say that I am not attracted to her at all. That doesn't matter; she's your wife, not mine. As long as you appreciate her beauty, that is all that matters.

She will not have a problem when I want to hang with the guys.

Hey guys, it's OK for us to hang out with our boys sometimes. But it doesn't have to be every weekend, quarterly, or even yearly. Most men who have a family and are on their grind don't really have time to hang out that much, anyway. As men, we should spend more time teaching our sons how to be men and our daughters how to be ladies and building our marriages.

We must be sexually compatible.

Yeah, this was right up there with being physically attractive on my list. Of course, you want to be with someone who you are sexually compatible with. Sex is very important in a marriage. It may not be the number one important thing, but I'm not going to lie, it was right up there in my top three. Why be with someone who only wants to have sex once a week when you are a three to four times a week kind of guy? Changes and compromises will always happen, but if you know you are not compatible in this area, some relationships may not make it.

She must know how to act in a social setting.

What do I mean by knowing how to act, you may ask? I'm glad you asked. Nothing is more embarrassing for a man than to take his girl out somewhere, and she doesn't know how to act. Arguing, talking loud, cussing, and fussing in public. Getting drunk and stumbling all over the place. Or when you take a lady to Chili's and she thinks you took her to an upscale restaurant. That shows me they have never been anywhere that they couldn't super-size. My wife will start clutching her pearls when she see's someone who can't hold their knife and fork correctly while cutting a steak. Hey, I'm sorry, but a man doesn't want to take you out if you haven't been socialized. If you are a dollar menu and a forty kinda girl, you should let a brotha know.

She will keep my secrets.

I tell my wife all the time that she is nosy. This woman will ask people whatever comes to her mind. I find myself giving her the look often. But she says if people didn't want me to ask questions, they wouldn't have started telling me the story. My wife is a good sounding board; she doesn't repeat things people tell her. Sometimes, men need our women to just listen. To be our sounding board. Listen to our hopes and to our dreams. We don't need you talking to all your friends and sharing the things that were just meant for your ears only. Pillow talk is for two. Unless there is a third head on your pillow, no one else should be a part of the conversation.

She must have a sense of humor

Ditto to what I said above; we laugh at each other and laugh with each other. And I must add, don't be super sensitive if you are the one being laughed at. Make sure it's all in love.

She must have her own dreams and goals.

This reminds me of the movie *Coming to America* with Eddie Murphy. He asked his potential wife what she liked. Her response was whatever he liked. What music do you listen to?

Whatever music you listen to. What's your favorite food? Whatever your favorite food is. We don't want a robot or someone exactly like us. Have your own dreams and goals separate from us. I didn't want to marry a clone of me. What do you want to accomplish? What is your five-year plan?

She must love God.

Yes, we want our women to love God just like y'all want us to love God. So, to this I would say ditto to what I said above. (I guess you would have to define what loving God means to you.)

She must be able to communicate without being super sensitive.

Y'all forever saying we need to talk. But when men do decide to talk and express how we feel about a certain subject, we don't want y'all to get all super sensitive. We don't want you wearing your feelings on your sleeve and taking everything so personal. Ladies, you can't keep pushing that we need to talk about a certain subject, and then, when we do talk about it, you don't like the outcome. Now, we have to deal with you being all in your feelings. I'm not saying that gives men license to be a jerk and insensitive. But please, just don't be so sensitive.

She can make her own money.

I'm not saying that she has to be the main breadwinner; I'm not even saying that what is mine is not hers. Some women don't even have to work outside the home. But men need to know that if something goes down and he's not working for a minute for whatever reason, that you can hold it down. (Sorry fellows, but no, I don't endorse the househusband thing. My opinion.) The list that men have is unnecessary, just like the ones that the women have. Let's take a look at the foundational requirement from scripture.

According to Proverbs 31:10 -11 (NIV), "A wife of noble character who can find? She is worth far more than rubies. Her husband has full confidence in her and lacks nothing of value."

Character and Confidence

A woman of character and confidence is a beautiful sight to behold. I understand that there has to be a mutual attraction on both sides. So, instead of using an exhaustive list, focus on core principals. Marriage is not a TV show or something you read in a romance novel; we don't get to rehearse our scenes, and there is no writer to hit the delete button or director to say cut. We all need to have realistic expectations, and we just might be surprised at the person that God will send our way

Chapter 9

DON'T GIVE UP ON YOUR MARRIAGE

A Lasting Groove

Ramona Jones

"Have You Prayed Together Today?"

"So, Jacob worked seven years to pay for Rachel. But his love for her was so strong that it seemed to him but a few days" (Genesis 29:20 NLT).

The Bible says in Genesis 29:18 KJV, "And Jacob loved Rachel; and said, I will serve thee seven years for Rachel thy younger daughter." Jacob worked seven years to pay for Rachel. He found his rib, and he was patient while doing what was needed in order to make her his wife. He said working seven years to get Rachel was like working a few days. (That's love.) For those of you who have read the story, poor guy ended up working fourteen years total.

Why is it that we work so hard to get married, but once we are married, we don't work just as hard to stay together? It really saddens me to see how marriage is looked upon now. People go into marriage like they are playing one of those escape room games. We go through each phase of our marriage looking for clues to get to the marriage escape door.

Stop giving up on your marriage. We can't enter marriage thinking the sun is always going to be shining and the birds will always be chirping. Sorry, but there are some winds and rainstorms we have to make our way through as well. If you live where they have wind and rainstorms, you know that you have to prepare for that season. You have to buy your hats, coats, gloves, Long Johns, etc. Just like you prepare for those stormy seasons, we also have to prepare for stormy seasons in our marriage. Don't get scared; all our marital storms won't be hail or "hell" storms. They may not even be thunder and lightning storms. Some might just be small windstorms blowing some of that stuff out of the way so we can see a new season coming.

How did we become a society where divorce is the normal and long-term marriages have become obsolete? People say it's a new day. The millennials are saying they don't need a piece of paper to define their love. And Generation Z has me so confused I can't even speak on them.

Yet from what I can see, people are still on the quest to find that special someone, the perfect love, their soul mate. We have dating websites, dating TV shows, matchmakers, and now, there are shows where we let an expert match us with a spouse we meet for the first time at the altar. How crazy is that? It's hard enough keeping a solid marriage with someone you have dated for months or years, but imagine marrying someone who you meet for the first time at the altar.

The first rule of finding the perfect love is to realize that no person is perfect. Other than God's love, there is no perfect love.

Why has divorce become an easier solution for us than working for our marriage? When there is a bump in the road, why do we convince ourselves that we need a break or that we are better alone? That was never God's plan. When we find that special someone and say the words I do, we must try to divorce proof our marriage.

"How?" you may ask. Well, I'm glad you asked. Divorce proofing takes hard work, time, communication, trust, love, tears, understanding, humbleness, and vulnerability. Did I say hard work?

We have to prepare for storms. We have to be prayed up. I don't care if you call on God, Jesus, or a higher power. When you get married, you are going to need something supernatural to help keep you from giving up when going through the storms of life and marriage.

I hate to see couples give up so easily, throw in the towel, and not even try to put up a fight for their marriages. If your marriage is worth fighting for, then fight for it. (Let me say that one more time. If your marriage is worth fighting for, then fight for it.)

I know some of you are reading this right now and saying *Ramona told me I need to fight for my marriage.* You won't even see the part about *if your marriage is worth fighting for.* Some marriages are not even worth fighting for. Some of us stay in loveless marriages and tolerate each other and make each other miserable.

Marriage sometimes can be like a roller coaster ride with ups and downs and sudden twists and turns. But if you hang on tight, you'll make it to the end of the ride safely. While we ride that coaster, we begin to understand the phrase "patience is a virtue." If you don't have the patience to deal with another person for more than your eight-hour shift at work, you are not ready for marriage. We have to decide not to give up on our marriage. Don't be so quick to walk away from your marriage. Don't convince yourself that the grass is greener on the other side. Because it's not. You've already been on the other side. You know what it's like. Don't be fooled into thinking that things have changed over there just because you got married. Single life is still the same; at some point, you need to retire your player card and turn on the water sprinklers on your side of the fence.

Divorce is hard. Please don't think it's easy. It can be very devastating. And not just for you. It can also be devastating for your children, in-laws, and friends. Remember, others have invested in your relationship as well. When you marry, you put your time, effort, love, and trust into this person. You've formed a marital bond that should not be broken. After a divorce, not only has the bond been broken, but you may also feel broken. You wonder if you will ever get past the pain that you are feeling. Now, you have to think about splitting material assets, bank accounts, and deciding who gets the kids on birthdays and holidays. This is why we must come up with ways to divorce proof our marriage. I will share a few.

Put God first.

First and foremost, we must put God first. God is the master builder. Build your relationships on a solid foundation. He wants us to live in unity and harmony. Make God the master of your home. God created marriage, and He can help us in those times when we feel like giving up.

Have patience.

Patience is the capacity to accept or tolerate and delay trouble or suffering without getting angry or upset. With the operative words being *without getting angry or upset*. We can't verbally say we're trying to be patient when our angry body language is screaming something totally different.

Within marriage, we can choose to be patient with each other, or we can choose to be angry all the time. Being patient in our marriage will cause us to think before we speak. We all have annoying little habits. Some of those things may never change. (Please don't think that you don't have any annoying habits. You are lying to yourself.) Learning to deal with our spouse's annoying habits is part of being patient. Remember, I said patience means the capacity to accept or tolerate.

Having patience with someone does not happen overnight. So, be prepared to lose patience sometimes. It's normal; we are all human. We all get angry. However, losing your patience does not mean that you have lost your mind. Take some deep breaths, and think before you speak. If possible, don't deal with the situation while you are angry because when we become impatient, we give impatient responses.

Never make your mate feel inadequate or incompetent.

Don't say or do things to make your mate feel incompetent

or inadequate. Take time to think about what you are going to say and how what you say will affect your mate.

No relationship is perfect; inevitably, your spouse is going to do something that will make you angry. I do things to make my husband angry all the time. One of my worst offenses is that I forget things. My husband may ask, "Babe, can you do me a favor and pick up the dry cleaning?"

I'll say, "OK, sure." When he gets home, he'll ask, "Did you get a chance to pick up the dry cleaning?" Sometimes my answer is "No, I forgot." He has one of two ways to handle the situation. He can be understanding. He may say, "Babe, I reminded you this morning to pick up the dry cleaning, and you still forgot." Or he can choose to make me feel incompetent and say, "What good are you? Every time I ask you to do something you forget." I can choose to say, "I'm sorry. I forgot. I'll get it tomorrow." Or I could say, "Next time, pick it up yourself."

Don't talk about your spouse's inadequacies to others. If your wife is a little ditsy, don't tell everyone that your wife can't handle business because she acts like a dumb blonde. If your husband doesn't like to watch or play sports, don't tell everyone he's not a real man. Let's build up, not tear down.

Hangout with other couples that have strong relationships.

Believe me, I know how difficult it can be to find another couple who both of you actually enjoy hanging out with. The whole "finding couple friends" is hard. One of you may not always like one or both of the people in the other couple. My husband and I go out with couples all the time. We enjoy being with other positive couples that we can gain something from or deposit something into. What's difficult is when you are always the one who is making the deposit. (Don't allow other couples to drain you with their marital issues.)

Be an open book.

Remember, we are divorce proofing our marriage. We have to be an open book. Be honest and trustworthy. Don't be sneaky. Don't have two cell phones, secret social media pages, and friends of the opposite sex that your spouse doesn't know about. We can't live secret lives outside of our marriage.

Don't bore each other.

I have noticed that couples say that they are bored with their spouse. One likes to travel, and the other doesn't. One likes to go out and socialize, and the other would rather stay home and watch movies. Once you start to get bored with your partner, that is an open door for a troubled marriage. When you start doing too many things without your spouse, you can slowly begin to drift apart. When you get bored with each other, it is easy to become roommates and married in name only. As I already said, I'm not OK with married couples taking a lot of vacations separate from each other. It's OK to take some trips away from your spouse, but I don't want to be looking at the beautiful blue waters of Jamaica and go back to my hotel and chill with my girls. Some of you may not agree with this, and that's OK. My book, my opinion.

Allow me to be me.

This was important to me when I got married. Some people will always try to change you into what they want you to be. Have you ever watched the movie *The Stepford Wives*? All the men wanted the perfect wife who cooked, cleaned, and made them feel like they were the best sexual partner she ever had. She agreed with everything he said and was always dressed up with impeccable makeup. Well, sorry, that ain't my testimony. I am not a Stepford Wife. I didn't sign up to be one. We must allow our spouses to be themselves. One of my daughters and one of my nieces have very loud laughs. They laugh so loud it's contagious. When you hear them laugh, it makes you want to laugh. If they were to marry someone who was embarrassed that they had boisterous laughs and told them that they should try to stifle their laugh, that person is not letting them be themselves. If I had to describe myself, I would say I am an introvert; who can become extrovert when needed. Although I can talk to anyone about anything, I like spending time alone. I read, write, journal thoughts, or just talk to God. My husband is more of an extrovert. But he never tried to change me. He never said, "Ramona, I wish you talked more, or I wish you were this or that way." He allowed me to be me, and I allowed him to be him. Be with someone who allows you to be you and loves you for who you are.

Enjoy date night.

I know this may be repetitive, but it's very important. So, I'll keep throwing it out there like a subliminal message. Make time to spend alone time together. I didn't just say spend time together. I said make time to spend alone together. People make time for things that are important to them. You need time as a couple away from the children. A time to just chill and say this is my woman, and this is my man. Not mommy, daddy, sister, brother, or employee just the two of you spending time connecting, talking, laughing, and enjoying each other's company. Find things you have in common, and make a date of it. We go hard after our careers and making money. We have children to tend to and other obligations. Make time to spend together. Take out a calendar if you have to, and pencil some time in. It may not be the most romantic way to do it, but make it happen. If you don't spend quality time together, you will eventually become roommates instead of a married couple. Don't get bored with each other.

Practice intimacy.

We already talked about intimacy in our marriage, so I won't repeat myself. You are not divorce-proofing your marriage if you are not making love. If you need more information, go back up and reread the romance and intimacy chapter.

Communicate. Don't bottle things up.

Communicate when you are happy, and communicate when you are sad. Don't keep your feelings all bottled up. Anger can be like a steaming pot; if the lid stays on tight when the pot begins to boil, eventually the top will pop off. If you are keeping your feelings bottled up inside, eventually you are going to pop off. You and your mate will not always agree on everything. But always make them aware of how you are feeling on a subject. Don't get to the point of divorce and then say I felt this way for a long time, but I just never said anything. Your bad. If you never said anything, how was your spouse supposed to know? You did not do your part in divorce proofing your marriage.

Know what you need from your marriage.

Some of us enter into marriage and are not really sure what we need from our marriage. You have to know what it is you need from your partner. How can you divorce them for not giving you what you need, when you never made your needs clear? (Let that sit for a minute.) Make it clear to your spouse what you need from your marriage. Your partner does not know what you need or what your expectations of the marriage are unless you communicate it to them. Tell them if what you need is companionship, trust, emotional safety, acceptance, financial safety, etc. It is our job to make our partner aware. Our spouses are not mind readers.

In my marriage, I wanted our home to be a place of peace. I would not have been divorce proofing my marriage if what I wanted was a peaceful marriage but married someone who believed that arguing and fighting was the way to solve our problems.

Don't take breaks from each other.

I know I said this before, and I'll say it again. When did it become OK to take a break from your marriage? What Einstein came up with that phrase, and why did everyone just adapt to it so easily? This is why we have all the paternity shows on the air trying to figure out who your baby's daddy is. On these shows, I hear them say, "Well, I'm not sure if it's my husband's baby or someone else's because we were on a break." You can't take a break from marriage. Either you are in or you are out. There is no in-between. There are no breaks in marriage. If you are tired of me, go in the living room.

Be careful with social media.

With modern technology making it so easy, we can now Facebook, Tweet, Instagram, or Link our way right into an affair. I hear so many couples telling me, "Ramona, my spouse and I don't have Facebook because it gets us in trouble." Sorry people, but it's not social media's fault. Social media was set up so that people could easily stay connected. Our friends and relatives can live in other states, and we can still share in each other's lives. So, when I hear people say they don't have Facebook because it breaks up relationships, it gives me pause. Facebook can't accept friends by itself; it cannot post hookup messages by itself. It can't search for old lovers by itself.

Your phone cannot give someone your phone number by itself; it cannot send text messages by itself, nor can it send nude pictures by itself. That's all you. Don't blame technology.

Here are some words of wisdom. Don't look up exes on your social media accounts. Think about the reason that the two of you broke it off back then. Nothing has changed. Stop looking backward. Y'all remember what happened in the Bible when Lot's wife looked back. Your ex is your past. Live in the future.

Don't have emotional affairs.

Sometimes, emotional affairs can happen before you are aware of what is going on. Don't get caught up. Make sure you know the signs; if you don't, here are a few of them.

- You start sharing things that should only be shared with your spouse.
- You start to make yourself visible to that person as much as possible.
- You start to dress to impress that person.
- You start to text or message that person more.
- When something good happens in your life, you want to share it with them.
- You can talk about sex freely with this person.
- You share with them negative things about your spouse.
- You display subtle PDA.

These little signs come about, and sometimes, we don't even notice them. I remember I was working at a company, and I became good friends with a guy. We took all of our lunches together and always talked. He was married, and I was married. There were times when his wife needed their car, and I would drop him off at home. He started calling me Ro instead of Ramona. I didn't think anything of it until my husband came to my job one day to take me to lunch, and I introduced him to my friend. Dude said to my husband, "Yeah, Ro is my girl, we go to lunch together every day. Now, you are here messing up our day." Then he proceeded to give my husband what came across as a challenging stare. Now, why did he have to do that?

Remember what I told y'all about knowing your spouse's crazy. Well one thing about my husband is, he has brown eyes. But when he gets sick or angry they turn a shade of hazel, so when I looked at his face and saw his eyes. I knew crazy had entered the building. All six foot eight inches of my husband got in this man's face and stared him down. Without a sign of a smile on his face, he told him, "My wife's name is Ramona, not Ro. In fact, I don't even want to hear you call her Ramona. You refer to her as Mrs. Jones from now on." The guy looked at my husband and then looked at me, as if I was going to correct him. Well I had to end that friendship because it seemed as if that guy was trying to make my husband think we meant more to each other than we did. Maybe I was a little slow on that one. I didn't notice that he was trying to take our friendship to a place it would have never gone. We sat in the lunchroom, we sat at the same table, and we talked. What did he think? Emotional affairs start off subtle. We have to pay attention. We must always be divorce proofing.

Keep others out of your marital business.

This is your marriage. No one understands how your marriage works except you and your spouse. What one person may not be able to deal with, another person can deal with for years. I always hear people say, "Wow, if I were you, I wouldn't put up with this or that." Then, there are those who want to give you advice and have never been married. Or they are in a bad relationship or divorced themselves. If you have that much advice, maybe you should have used it to save your own marriage. Remember, misery loves company.

Communicate.

Talk, Talk, and again, I say talk. Then listen. Listening is a very important part of communication. Sometimes, we talk so much and never take time to listen; this is why we don't understand our mate's needs. They've expressed their needs to us on several occasions, but we never listen. Don't just hear. *Listen.* We say I hear you. Yes, you may very well hear them speaking. But are we listening to what they are saying? It is also important to know your partner's nonverbal communication cues; notice the difference in tone and volume of their voice, gestures, facial expressions, and body posture.

Continue to get to know the person you married.

Throughout our marriage, we will continue to learn new things about our spouse. Of course, we will know the normal things that our spouse likes and dislikes, but over the years, people change. Their views change, their needs change, their dreams change, and their goals change. Continue to get to know the person you are married to. You must talk to each other and listen, not hear. (As I said, there is a difference.) I would hate it if another woman knew my husband's dreams for the future, and I didn't have a clue. I would hate to hear him say, "Babe, I told you this already." This means that I may have heard him, but I wasn't listening. But that other woman was listening.

Get to know what your spouse will and will not tolerate in your marriage. Get to know their moods; we all have moods. Good, bad, or indifferent, we have moods. Women, know what your man expects of a wife. Men, know what your woman expects of a husband. Never get too busy doing you that you stop getting to know one another.

Gold diggers don't just carry purses.

Comedian Sheryl Underwood used to tell a joke where she would say she was a gold digger and carried her shovel in her purse. I won't lie. When I was young and single, I lived by that model. If a man was not already accomplished, he didn't need to bother looking my way. But just like some women or looking for a sugar daddy, some men are looking for women so that they can be taken care of as well. Don't just marry for money. If you marry for money, that is the only thing you have in common. If the money runs out, the relationship will run out. There will be nothing else that will keep the two of you together.

Don't call each other out of your names.

I can't understand how you are divorce proofing your marriage when you fight and cuss each other out. I don't know about y'all, but it would be very difficult for me to go from being called b——h to now being called baby. I don't care how angry you are, you can control what comes out of your mouth. The only time you should call your spouse out of their name is if it is a term of endearment.

Don't get physical.

It's OK to be physical and put our hands on each other in a loving way. But don't put your hands on each other in anger. Keep your hands to yourself. This goes for both parties; women are not the only ones to get physically abused. If you are that angry where you feel like you want to physically harm one another, you need to take a beat. You need to leave the room, walk out of the house, or do whatever you need to do to deescalate the situation.

Let's stay in this thing for the long haul and make it a sweet groove. Work on ways together to divorce proof your marriage.

Chapter 10

YOURS, MINE, AND OURS

EXTENDED FAMILIES AND FRIENDS

A Family Groove

Ramona Jones

"Have You Prayed Together Today?"

"Beloved, let us love one another, for love is from God, and whoever loves has been born of God and knows God" (1 John 4:7 ESV).

Have you ever heard the phrase *you don't just marry your spouse, but you marry their whole family*? And please, don't forget all the friend-in-laws. Just like we can't pick our own family, we can't pick our extended family or our friend-in-laws.

Darryl and I are blessed that we get along well with each other's family members and most of the friends. We don't always agree on everything with our perspective families. Most of us have very strong personalities, so we bump heads sometimes. Even with disagreements and head bumping, we have learned to agree to disagree and continue to be there for one another, spend time together, and love one another. I have two sisters and one brother. My husband has five sisters and two brothers. Our families are very different. But it doesn't matter what side of the family we are with, we always have a great time.

When we get married, our families are combining; we must remember we are entering into a new family. And although we are now a part of our spouse's family, we have to remember that our spouse's family may do things differently than our own family. We know how to deal with our own family in different situations. We can talk to our family a certain way, we can joke with our own family a certain way, and our own family member may not see anything wrong.

But our spouse's family may not like it and see it as you being disrespectful to them if we spoke or joked with them in the same manner as we speak to our own family. We have to get to know our extended family. I'm sorry to be the one who has to tell you this, but you won't always be liked by your extended family. And some of our spouse's friends may hate us more than their family members do.

Family and friends can test the ties that bind. This is why, as husband and wife, we must decide together how we feel about dealing with situations concerning extended family. We have to set rules and boundaries.

I remember my husband and I were babysitting for our

youngest daughter. Each time my husband would try to sit down, our grandson, who was two years old at the time, would jump in the seat first. My husband would look at him, laugh, and say, "Boundaries, Darryl."

Darryl, who has the same name as his papa, would repeat, "Boundaries, Papa."

The same applies to family members. We have to set boundaries and rules together as a couple. (I know. There goes that word rules again.) I understand how we feel about that five-letter word, but like I already said, we all have to live by somebody's rules.

When it comes to extended family members, we should come to an agreement and set the rules. And we are to make sure we both understand the agreement and the rules of how family situations should be addressed and what boundaries we should set. I know we can't possibly come up with every scenario that may occur in our families, nor will we have a solution as to how we are going to deal with every scenario. But we should talk about the basics. I will name just a few of what I consider the basic scenarios that happen in almost every family.

Family members dropping by unannounced.

Some families and friend's hangout all the time. They do dinners, birthdays, holidays, and they take vacations together. These family members and friends are used to dropping by any day and any time unannounced because that was the way they always did it when we were single. Now that we are married, we have to think about the way our spouse's feel about all the family togetherness. Our spouse may not be used to someone just dropping by anytime they are in our area. Let's keep it real some of our spouses just don't want to see our family and friends every day.

This is where communication needs to take place. You have to discuss what is and is not acceptable for your household as far as friends and family is concerned. When my husband and I first got married, one of my sisters would come to our house every day. I had just had our youngest daughter, so I was home. Sometimes, I needed the adult conversation, so it really didn't bother me much. She would come early and not leave until my husband came home. My husband said to me once, "Babe, I don't mind your sister coming over, but does she have to come every day?" Then he said, "Better yet, can she leave sometimes before I come home?" It wasn't that he didn't like or love my sister, it was that he wanted to come home to his wife and his children and not his wife, children, and sister-in-law every day.

If you have a spouse that doesn't mind people saying, "I was just in the neighborhood so I dropped by," then cool. That works for you. But for me, I prefer a heads up. Sometimes, when you are at home relaxing, relaxing is what your body needed. So, I'm not a real big fan of the pop-up visit. Whatever criteria you have set for your household, the time will come when each spouse separately will have equal responsibility to let their separate friends and family know the rules of your household.

When the time comes, you have to make one of your family members or friends aware of the rules of your household. Make sure you tell them in a way that won't cause contention between them and your spouse. (This is very important.) Don't tell your family member, "My husband or my wife said you come over too much." Now, they have hurt feelings, and they are saying, "I won't come over anymore." Now your family member is mad at you and hates your spouse.

Loaning family members money.

I hear people say all the time, "I only loan what I can afford to give away." But let's keep it real: yes, we may have been in the position to give that loan. But we all like getting our money back. We should discuss with our mate what is an appropriate amount to loan to a family member. I am aware that in marriage a lot of us have our own personal bank accounts, and every now and then, we can sneak a loan to momma, sister, brother, or friend. But this is not always a good practice and eventually can become problematic. If you made the loan without telling your mate, your family member may expect you to continue to sneak them money.

Additionally, don't loan money that is needed for your bills or something important in your household without your spouse's knowledge, not even if your family member assured you that it would be paid back before you actually need it. Don't put your household at risk trying to help someone else's household. What if they are unable to return the money in the promised time frame? They'll tell you, "Sorry, it's not my fault that the money didn't come when I thought it would come." Now, this is going to cause major problems in your marriage. So, make sure you follow the lending guidelines of your household.

Allowing family to move in.

My husband and I live in the downtown area of Long Beach, California. In the area that we live, a lot of different events are hosted. We live near hotels, so there is always a conference going on. We also live near the beach, so there is always the beach crowd. There is also the Long Beach Jazz Festival yearly and a host of other events. So, family is always asking to crash at our place for different events. This is something my husband and I don't mind. Our home has always been a place of peace.

No matter where I live, I always like my home to be a place of peace. I like people to feel like they are almost on a mini vacation when they stay overnight. Heck, I might even cook you a meal. (Now, did y'all notice I said mini-vacation and stay overnight?). But you gotta go home. As much as I love family and friends to come for a visit, I also love to see family leave. *(Geeeetttt ouuuuuttttt.)*

When it comes to allowing family members to move into our homes long-term or short-term, it is a discussion that should never be taken for granted. Sometimes, family members fall on hard times and need our help. Try not to take on the attitude that this is my house just as much as it's my spouse's, so if my family member needs to stay here, it should be OK. Sorry, but it's not always OK.

It's imperative that you have a discussion with your spouse about family moving in. You may think. *My spouse really likes my family member or friend and gets along well with them.* But that does not mean that they want them in their home every day.

When we allow someone to move into our home, we must understand that everyone in the house has to get used to the change. There is another person in our home. They don't know all the rules of our home. You may like people to take their shoes off when they enter your home. No smoking, no drinking, no guests, or no pets.

At a certain time of the evening, I like to chill. I don't know about ya'll (talking to my ladies) but when I'm chillin, I like to get super comfortable. I take my shoes off, makeup off, and bra off. (And not exactly in that order because the bra may go before the shoes.) When you have a houseguest, your chill is a little different; the bra can't come off until you go into your bedroom. Having someone else in our home is not always an easy adjustment. But once the decision has been made and both of you agree to allow this move to take place and welcome our family member into our home, the very next conversation we should have is with that family member.

This conversation is of the utmost importance; it must take place, and it must take place prior to them moving into our home. During this conversation, two very important things must be talked about. (Highlight this part. No, really. I'm serious.) Never allow family or friends to move into your home without first setting a time frame for their intended stay. You are wondering how long they plan to stay, but they think the invitation is open-ended. Never say stay as long as you need or until you get back on your feet (Unless you really mean it). As long as someone needs can mean a few weeks or a month to you. But to them, it can mean days, months, or even years. Some family members go as far as asking if they can just start paying you a little something and stay indefinitely.

Secondly, let them know upfront the rules of your household. Some people may say, "I'm grown. I'm not going by any rules." Well, you were grown when you came to live here, and you are going to be grown while walking out my door. Don't allow others to disturb your peace.

Parents with adult children.

Adult children tend to think that their parent's door should always be open to them. It's OK to assist our adult children. But we don't have to allow the door to our home to become a revolving door for our adult children. If we do, they will never become self-sufficient adults. They will always know that if they can't make it on their own, or if they just don't like their job anymore because they didn't make manager in three months, they can quit and just come home. Or if they are on a break with their girlfriend or boyfriend, they might say, "I'll just stay at my parent's house for a little while." At some point, we have to push our little birdies out of the nest so they can fly. Some parents don't mind their adult children coming back home, but make sure both of you are on the same page. You raised your children; unless it's absolutely necessary, don't start raising your grandchildren, too. (It's called empty nester for a reason. Time to enjoy you. You do deserve it.)

Even more concerning is when parents move into their adult children's homes. Sometimes, the husband or wife resort back to childlike behaviors, and we actually allow our parents to become the head of our households. We allow them to tell us how to cook, clean, deal with our spouse, and rear our children. This should never happen. You are an adult now. Our parents are a guest in our home. Therefore, it is our responsibility to make sure that our families, friends, and parents always respect us and our spouse in our homes.

Having Family in your marital business.

Never let family come between you and your spouse. Now, don't get me wrong, I'm not telling you to never discuss your marriage issues with your family because, realistically, we all need to vent at times. But we must be careful what we decide to share with family and which family members we choose to share with. Sorry to tell you this, but you can't share things with some family. Some family will always make mountains out of molehills.

If your spouse did something wrong and you shared it with a family member, yes, you are upset and venting your frustrations. But after you and your spouse talk it over, you might decide to let the offense go. You forgive your spouse and move on. Keep in mind your family may never forgive them, and they will continue to question you for forgiving them. Of course, you love your family members and respect their opinion, but it should always be up to you whether or not to forgive. Women, never let another woman tell you that you should leave your man. Sometimes, your friend may be looking out for you, but sometimes that woman may be jealous of what you have. In some cases, she may want what you have. And men should never let another man tell him you should leave your woman. Whatever the offense was, when it comes to leaving your spouse, that should be something you thought long and hard about and made the decision on your own.

How to handle holidays.

Another thing that we sometimes forget about when it comes to family and marriage are those wonderful holidays and where they will be spent. This may sound like a simple thing that you don't need to talk about. But believe me, that is far from the truth. She may be used to spending every holiday with her family while he wants to spend holidays with his family. Whichever way you decide to go, the other family may get mad or have hurt feelings. Come up with some sort of agreement. Christmas at his parent's house and Thanksgiving at your parent's house one year.

Switch it around the following year. Family always believes that your new spouse is the cause of the changes in the family tradition. So, there may be some bad feeling between spouses and their in-laws. It is still up to you and your spouse to define boundaries with your families when it comes to your marriage. You may not want to spend the holidays with either family. I remember when our children got older and moved out of our home and had their own families, my husband and I decided we would do Thanksgiving and Easter with either of our families, and we would travel for Christmas. It wasn't a popular decision with either of our families. Guess what? It's OK. Do you. Some may not like it, but they have to respect the decision you and your spouse made.

Dealing with family and your spouse.

This may be hard to hear, but your family may never like your spouse. Your spouse may never like them. If it don't fit, don't force it. Don't try to force your spouse to do things and spend holidays with your family when they make it very clear that they don't like them. If at all possible, don't allow anyone to make your spouse feel uncomfortable; your spouse and your marriage should take priority. However, just because your spouse and family don't get along, it should never stop you from visiting your family without your spouse. Never cut ties with your family just because they don't like your spouse. But never allow your family to speak negatively about them to you. When we visit our family and friends and they want to talk badly about our spouse, let them know upfront that it is not acceptable. If it continues, this is when you will have to make a decision about if you want to continue to hangout with them.

Couples, make sure you have discussions about these topics, and hold each other accountable to what was agreed upon.

Chapter 11
WORK HARD, PLAY HARD

Enjoy Your Spouse

A Balance Groove

Ramona Jones

"Have You Prayed Together Today?"

"May your fountain be blessed, and may you rejoice in the wife of your youth" (Proverbs 5:18 NIV).

Work hard, play hard. (repeat.)

Work and play balance can sometimes be very difficult to manage. Some people have a hard time balancing the two. But it is very important to achieve balance between work and play. My husband has always been a workaholic. He enjoys working. Over the years, he has been blessed with careers that he has loved. When I am working outside of the home, my schedule can become hectic as well. However, I have always known how to plan family activities. I also know how to let my husband know when I need some honey time.

Sorry, y'all. I don't have a simple solution for creating the work to play balance in your family. Every family is different. We have different schedules and different needs. But we all share a common goal. We are all on the grind, working hard to achieve the dream. That's why, sometimes, we have to step away from the grind and play.

Most of us work forty or more hours per week. Some commute for hours or travel for work. Some of us love our careers. For others, it's just a job. Whichever the case may be, always be thankful that you have a job to help support your household. When you go to your job, work hard, and try to do your job well. Be the best you that you can be at your position. There is nothing wrong with working hard. We are supposed to work to provide for ourselves and to have all the things we need. We also work hard to have the things we just flat-out want.

The problem we run into is managing our free time. On our days off from work, we allow ourselves to get busy running errands that we didn't have time to do during our workweek. We become Uber for our kid's sports, practices, and other activities. If you're anything like me, the chair in our bedroom is full of clothes that I didn't hang up from my work week. So, we spend our weekend hanging up clothes, taking clothes to the cleaners, or washing clothes.

And let's not forget those extended family and friend functions that we simply must attend like baby showers, wedding showers, weddings, BBQ's, and do we really have to attend every church function that we are invited to. I don't know about y'all, but sometimes I just don't want to go to all that stuff. Sometimes, we just have to say, "Sorry y'all, we won't be coming to that. Yes, I want to play on my off days. I just don't feel like playing with y'all." We should take the time to break up the hustle and bustle of our everyday work schedules and make time to play with each other.

Learning how to balance work and play is a necessity in order to have a balanced relationship. My husband always makes the comment that people make time for the things that are important to them. After God, your marriage should be your primary relationship. It should be important enough for you to make time for it. You should make time to enjoy each other.

I have found over the years that in order to find the time we need for each other, we all need to master the fine art of saying no. It's a very simple word, *no*. No, I can't work overtime. No, I can't babysit your children. No, I can't take you to an appointment. No, I can't attend your function. No, I can't listen to you talk about how miserable you feel your life is for an hour. Just no. *No*. That small two letter word packs a lot of power. Mastering the fine art of saying no will free up so much of our time. Try it. You will find it to be so freeing and liberating. Just say no.

Now, it's time to play! If you have children, playing and vacationing with the children is important. We need to have family fun. But equally important is the time we spend playing and relaxing with our mate. I love hanging out with my husband. He's fun and he's funny, and we always have good conversations. We are big foodies, so we like to go out for dinner or find a new brunch spot. Our favorite thing to do on nice hot days is have a beach day. And when I say beach day, I mean beach day. We have our chairs, hats, sunscreen, blanket, tent, books, music, and food. I mean, it's an all-day event. Some people say they only go to the beach and walk on the pier. Nope. We like to stick our feet in the sand and wade in in the water. It's so relaxing. If you are not playing, let's get started. Find something fun you both like doing and play.

Set date nights.

Set a date night. It can be once a week, once every other week, or once a month. Date night should just be for you and your mate. It should be time to spend together and enjoy each other's company away from home. Date nights don't have to be expensive. Go for a walk, take a drive, have an inexpensive lunch at a local spot, or sit at the park or beach and talk. Take an Uber to a nice spot, and have a glass of wine if that's your thing. (Uber is your designated driver.)

It is imperative that you set aside time to do things alone as a couple; this is the way we maintain closeness. Never go months without spending time alone as a couple. Just because you live in the same house and you see each other daily does not mean you are spending quality time together. I'm talking about taking a detour from the norm. We must never forget how to enjoy each other.

Go out with other couples.

It's cool to go out with like-minded couples and couples that genuinely like each other. It's fun to go out with another couple that enjoys some of the things that we enjoy. Like I said above, Darryl and I are foodies, and we love the beach. When other couples want to hang out with us, we must make sure they are like-minded. Don't let other couples disturb your groove.

Vacations or staycations.

Take vacations/staycations together. Going to every church convention or conference that comes up is not a vacation. For my Pastors visiting another Pastors church when you are on vacation, is not vacation. Most times you will be asked to give the word, say a few words, pray or collect the offering

Don't make excuses.

People come up with millions of excuses as to why they don't play hard. "We don't have anyone to watch our children" is one of the biggest excuses couples use for not spending time alone and having fun together. In some cases, we don't have a babysitter because we never bothered to ask. Try asking a family member or friend. You may be surprised; sometimes, they will say yes. One thing my children know well about their mother is I have no problem babysitting my grandchildren. But I don't like last-minute babysitting. Don't call me Saturday morning asking if I can babysit Saturday night unless it is an emergency. Remember, mama got a life too. Let me know a couple weeks in advance. When we are empty nesters, we have to get our minds prepared for the babies that touch everything, the teens with the teen attitudes, and the special eaters who only eat certain things. So, give us the consideration of prior notice.

When looking for a sitter, we can also go on a babysitting website and interview some sitters. Technology makes it easy for us. We can use that same technology to set up nanny cams. You can get out together for a few hours and also keep an eye on your little one. Stop making excuses.

We don't have money to go out.

Couples have said to me, "Ramona, we would love to go out and do things as a couple like you and Darryl, but we don't have money to go out." Going out or just spending quality time together does not have to cost a whole lot of money. Get creative.

- Go on a picnic with food from your fridge.
- Download a game you can play together, or go old school: play video games, cards, or dominos. Or how about a naughty game of twister?
- Go to car lots and test drive cars.
- Go to open houses and walk through houses you may never be able to afford. (We love doing this. We've been doing this ever since we got married.)
- Go on a hike.
- Find free movies or concerts in the park.

Sorry, y'all; if you say you are not spending quality time with your mate because of finances, it may be that you just don't want to spend time together.

Laugh together.

When you get the opportunity to spend time together alone, try not to spend your whole night out talking about children and family members and friends. (I have one caveat to that statement. If talking about children, family, and friends causes you to laugh, then it's OK.) It's so important to laugh together. And sometimes, talking about family and friends can always give you some of the best laughs. It's OK to laugh together and be silly together. Have private jokes that only the two of you understand. My husband can make me laugh so hard sometimes I'll be in tears.

Ask yourself this. Is your mate making you cry sad tears more than tears from laughter? (I'm just gon' leave that right there.)

If you are not spending quality time together, start today. I'm not saying spend all your free time together because that would be an impossible request. Couples, if you are not already doing it, start dating. Reconnect. Talk, talk, and I again say talk. Why do some of us live in the same home with our spouse and feel lonely? This should not be. If a bond was broken, see if it can be restored. We didn't get married to feel like a single person.

In marriage, you have to continually get to know each other. My husband and I are not the same people who got married over thirty years ago. People change hopes and dreams change. I have heard people say they grew apart. That the mate they married no longer completes them. Yeah, it was sweet when Tom Cruise told his female co-star that she completed him. But this is real life. Sure, couples can outgrow each other, but most of the time, it's because they just stopped trying. You stopped doing things together, and you stopped sharing your hopes and dreams. You stopped making love, laughing, and playing together.

We spend forty hours or more a week working. So, when we have free time, we shouldn't just think about hanging out with our friends and doing things apart from our spouse. I look on social media and see couples posting fun events and vacations separate from their spouse all the time. Again, I'm not saying that you have to do everything together. But when I see most of their free time is spent apart, a bond has been broken. Or the bond was never formed.

I see married women on social media posting pictures of exotic vacations. But they are on these vacations with their girlfriends. Sure, it's cool for ladies to go on girls' trips, and it's also cool for our husband to go on vacation with the boys. Just not all the time.

Make the decision today that we are going to build a play together bond, or we are going to re-build the bond we once had. Make it a priority to make plans to do something together. We live in an electronic gadget world where we can plan activities without leaving the comfort of our homes. Start today. Someone in the relationship has to take the lead on this. Don't just work hard, make time to play hard. This is a must for a strong relationship. Work hard so you can play harder.

Chapter 12

FIGHT FAIR

A Power of Wills Groove

Ramona Jones

"Have You Prayed Together Today?"

"Death and life are in the power of the tongue: and they that love it shall eat the fruit thereof" (Proverbs 18:21 KJV).

My parents fought regularly when I was young, but they stayed married for years. It makes me think of a song that came out in the seventies called "Thin Line Between Love and Hate" by The Persuaders. I was a young girl when it was released, so I really didn't understand the meaning of the words to this song. As I grew and started to enter into relationships of my own, it all made since.

Let's keep it real. Being married is not always going to be a walk in the park. We all have fights. I'm not referring to physical fights. (Although some of y'all might do that as well.) What I'm referring to are verbal disagreements. And let me tell you, a verbal disagreement is just as bad, if not worse, as a physical altercation. In a verbal disagreement, we can go for the jugular with words. If you go for my jugular when we fight, you have crossed a thin line between love and hate because our words were not just meant to hurt. Life and death are in the power of the tongue. So, let's learn to fight fair.

I have a strong personality, and I never wanted a yes-man in my life. Believe me when I tell you, I didn't get one. I am the youngest sister of three girls, and we have a younger brother. My sisters and I are all very strong-willed women. My husband always says you have to be a strong man to be married to a Wood's woman (our maiden name).

Like I said in an earlier chapter, my husband is a gentle giant, but he can become a roaring bear. Becoming a roaring bear is not a reason to fight unfairly. Because we are roaring and angry, we still need to be conscious of what is coming out of our mouths. Words hurt; they can feel equal to being slapped across the face, or worse.

When we were young in our marriage and Darryl and I would have a disagreement about something, we would debate back and forth. Then he would pause for several seconds before responding. Later in our marriage, I figured out that he would pause so he could figure out a way to respond without going for the jugular. He wanted to fight fair. It took me a while to learn this. I always fought to win.

As a couple, we can get into arguments and say things to each other that are so hurtful I often wonder how we are going to recover from this. Some relationships will recover; some will never get past the things that were said. When misunderstandings happen, and they will. I have rules for fighting. I know it may sound strange to have rules for fighting because when we are mad and we are fighting, rules go out the window. You just want to say what you want to say. Like me, you want to win. But when we think about it, winning isn't always a good thing. So, I give you these pointers. All of these points are important and come in no particular order.

***DJ.** When you and your mate fight, know what you are fighting about and stick to that. Don't get off subject with the "remember what happened two years ago, it was a Thursday night and it was raining. I was wearing green, and you were wearing blue." What does that have to do with the fight we are having today? Don't bring up past arguments. Stick to the issue at hand. It is so important to stay on topic when you are discussing a matter.

We have to be an active listener to the subject at hand. When I say active listener, I mean look at each other and don't start thinking about how you want to respond before the other has finished their thought. We all need the assurance that we are being heard and that what we have to say has value. When Ramona is expressing herself, I am quiet, but I give her eye contact and nod my head so that she knows that I am actively listening.

Once we have both expressed ourselves on the topic, only

then can we start trying to find a middle ground or a compromise. When it comes to problem solving, as mentioned before, I am a "bottom line" type of guy. I want to know what the problem is, and then, I can come up with possible solutions no emotions, just the facts. Wrong! That does not work with my wife. She wants to express how she feels and how what happened made her feel. I had to learn how to listen in a way that assures her that I am not trying to rush to the bottom line to solve it. Many times, she just wants to let me know how a certain thing that I did or said made her feel. There are times that she just wants to vent, and then, we are able to discuss the subject matter and come to a resolution. The key here is to work on your listing skills and work on staying on one topic at a time.

***Thanks for the input, honey.** I guess it's OK if he keeps jumping into my chapters. Like I already said, he's always all up in my space. Now, to my points.

Never get physical.

As a child, my parents physically fought, and it happened in our home more often than not. I still to this day wonder why it took them so long to separate. I believe the scar of seeing my parents physically fight still hasn't healed. When I see a man and woman physically fight, the little kid in me still wants to run and hide in the closet. Physical abuse is never OK. Women, we don't want him to put his hands on us, so we shouldn't put our hands on him. If someone is causing us to be so angry that we have to put our hands on him or her in a violent way, our issue is much deeper than a misunderstanding. Maybe we should consider counseling or going our separate ways. Fighting not only destroys your relationship, but it also destroys your children's faith in healthy relationships. If you don't care about yourselves, please think about the children.

Don't have revenge fights.

One time you made a mistake, and it caused an argument. A few months later, your mate makes the same or a similar mistake. Here's your chance. You are rubbing your hands together, smiling, and thinking, *I'm going to get my revenge today, and I'm going to let them have it*. It was a mistake when you did it, and it's a mistake when they did it. We all make mistakes.

Try not to yell.

When Darryl and I first got married, I used to yell at the top of my lungs when I was angry with him. This was learned behavior. I did not know the meaning of fighting fair. Remember, learned behavior can be unlearned. Now, I absolutely can't tolerate someone yelling at me. If you have something you need to say to me, say it. My hearing is very good. You do not need to raise your voice to get my attention. I realize that sometimes when we are angry, we feel that yelling is the only way our mate will actually pay attention to what we are saying. If you are yelling and they are yelling, is anybody truly listening? Just because you can say it the loudest doesn't make it right.

***DJ.** If you are not able to discuss the matter without yelling, wait or postpone the conversation until you can discuss it calmly. When we were first married, Ramona would yell, and then I would look at her and wait for her to complete her thoughts. I would talk in a calm voice, and I am sure she wandered why I was not yelling. Did I care? Why didn't I engage? I made a conscious decision that I was not going to communicate that way, which caused her to start communicating with me the same way as I was communicating with her.

Thanks Honey..Don't already have an answer before the question is finished.

I really hate when people say I already know what you are

going to say. No, you don't, and if you do, just let me finish my statement. When you have an answer for every question, it seems rehearsed. It's hard to know if you are telling the truth or just have thought of every conceivable scenario and planned an answer.

Don't hit below the belt.

We usually know what our mate's weaknesses are. Our mates should feel comfortable enough with us to be vulnerable. Don't use their weaknesses to hurt them in a fight; like I said, don't go for the jugular.

Don't call each other out of your names.

It's simple. Don't cuss each other out. How can you call the person that you say you love every bad word under the sun and expect them to be OK? Yes, sticks and stone will break your bones, but words will break your heart, spirit, and self-esteem.

Don't fight in front of your children.

Fighting in front of your children is very scary for them. They never get used to it. It affects them in different areas of their lives. It affects the way they look at you as their parents, the way they act in school, and the friends and mates they choose. Although some subscribe that fighting in front of our children is healthy to teach them that no relationship is perfect, I don't subscribe to that theory. Children have enough to deal with just being children. The last things a child needs on their young minds are the issues and problems of their parents. Like I said, my parents fought in front of my siblings and I all the time. Most times, it became physical. Growing up watching my parents fight had my young mind thinking that this is the way all marriages were supposed to be. How can we be an example to our children if all they see is a dad and mom disrespecting each other or hear one parent talking about the other to their friends and relatives negatively? Leave the children out of the drama.

Keep others out of your fights.

Stop dragging others into your fights. Mom, dad, sibling, friends, and all your social media friends do not want to be a part of your fight. Keep other people out of your business. Why have we become a society where we have to get everyone's opinion on decisions we make about our own life? If we don't get a like, emoji, or an opinion, we act as if we can't make a decision.

Don't take breaks.

The whole "we are on break" thing is foreign to me. A young lady asked me once how long I had been married. At that time, it had been twenty-seven years. She asked me, "In all those years, how many times have y'all taken a break?" When you take a break from your marriage, it gives others an opportunity to damage or break your marital bond. When taking breaks, we act as if we are single again and sometimes make bad decisions. You don't get to take breaks from marriage. Either we are together or we are not. Just because we have a fight, we don't get to leave and take a break from being married.

Don't sleep apart.

When you fight, don't sleep apart. Couples do their most bonding in the bedroom. If we keep telling our mate to go sleep on the couch or go to sleep in the guest room, eventually, they will start going willingly or they will find another bed that will welcome them in.

Pray for your marriage.

At the beginning of each chapter I ask, "have you prayed together today?" Take time daily and pray together for your marriage. Pray that God strengthens your marriage. Pray for unity. Pray for understanding; pray for love. Pray for peace, and pray you learn how to fight fair. Remember, prayer changes things.

Chapter 13
MY SPOUSE, MY FRIEND

A Friendly Groove

Ramona Jones

Darryl (DJ) Jones

"Have You Prayed Together Today?"

"As iron sharpens iron,
so a friend sharpens a friend" (Proverbs
27:17 NLT).

***DJ**. According to Dictionary.com, a friend is one attached to another by affection or esteem. My wife is my friend, my best friend. If I have the choice of spending my free time with anyone, she is the first person that comes to my mind. Why? Because she gets me. She understands me. Our souls are knitted together. After thirty-five years of marriage, she can read me. We can take a car ride together for hours and not say a word. Just placing my hand on her leg, that smile, or wink of the eye is like an entire conversation.

She knows me better than anyone. Sometimes, she will ask me if I am alright, and I'll say I am fine. She knows that I am not fine, but she also knows that sometimes I need to process my thoughts. So, she will give me time to do so. Don't get me wrong, she is not going to let me get away with "being fine" for days. She will say, "I know you are not fine, so when you are ready to discuss it, let me know". That means I have another day at the most before she starts pressing. Now, that is a friend. She understands the way that I process information, but she is not going to let me go on like this endlessly.

Before she became my wife, the mother of my children, my lover, and my confidant, she was my friend. We are still friendly with each other. Friends care for one another, and friends push each other to improve. Friends are some of your biggest supporters. I greatly value the friendship that I have with my wife.

***Ramona.** We hear people say it all the time. "I married my best friend. Should a husband and wife really be best friends?" Well, I don't have a right or wrong answer to that question. My husband is so much more than a best friend to me.

Prior to marriage, you both had friends that you hung out with all the time. When we first get married, we'd say we were never going to let go of our boys or our girls. And you shouldn't. Our friends should always remain a part of our lives. But once we are married, we have to prioritize where they fit into our new lives. Sorry husbands, you can't go smoke cigars and play pick-up games with the boys every weekend, and wives, we can't possibly think that we are going to continue to hang out with our girls and attend every girls' trip and every paint and sip event that pops up.

Our friends will always be a part of us. They will be there for happy and sad moments that occur in our lives. They will be there for graduations, weddings, baby showers, and funerals. But when we are married, hanging out with our friends too much can sometimes cause problems in our relationships. When we get married, sometimes it's hard for our friends to accept that they have to take second place to our spouse. And heaven forbid us saying something to our friends about them still wanting to have priority in our lives. Because now, we have to hear, "Since you got married, you changed; you're not like you were back in the day." Of course, you are not the same. You have different responsibilities now.

We don't have as much time to get caught up in all the friend drama. Let's face it, friends come with friend drama. Now, I'm not saying we stop caring about what's going on in our friends' lives just because we got married. But we can't allow friend drama to bring negativity into our marriage. We must strive to keep our marriage as drama free as possible, especially with other people's drama. Some women have many girlfriends, and they share every detail of their lives with the girls. I don't have a lot of girlfriends. I have two sisters, six sisters-in-laws, two adult daughters, a daughter-in-law-in-waiting and four granddaughters. That is way more than enough female interaction for my life.

Like I said, I don't have a right or wrong answer to the question of if your spouse should be your best friend or not. But for me, my husband is my best friend, and we happen to enjoy spending time together. Someone recently said to me, "Of course you guys enjoy spending time together: you have been together over thirty years." This is not always true. I know couples that have been together just as long or longer. They live together, work, and share all the expenses. They've accomplished the American dream together of family, careers, homes, cars, and vacations. They have been married for decades, but they are not friends.

When they have free time, they would rather spend it with anybody else other than spending time with their spouse. I think it is important to be friends with the person you have vowed your life to. Your spouse should be the person who knows you as well as you know yourself. When you are with your spouse, you should feel comfortable to be yourself. Having your spouse as your friend should be a relaxing experience. This is the person who should not be judgmental. Ladies, this is the person that you can take off your makeup, wig, bra, and Spanx around and just be you.

When your spouse is your friend, you become in sync with each other. You start to pick up each other's habits. You have favorite TV shows and inside jokes that only both of you understand. My husband and I always quote scenes from movies and laugh. Like I said, people always say we are corny. That's OK; it's good to be corny with your best friend.

When your spouse is your best friend, you have favorite things that you do together that wouldn't feel the same if you did them with someone else. They become the first person you want to tell when something good happens and the one whose shoulder you cry on when sad things happen. They are the person who will understand your good and bad days and accept your flaws. They are the person who knows when no words are needed and you just need a hug. Some of you may get everything I mentioned from other friends. But as for me, I like getting them from my best friend, my husband.

Chapter 14
THE MAN'S ROLE

A Man's Groove

Darryl (DJ) Jones

"Have You Prayed Together Today?"

"So, God created man in his own image,
in the image of God he created him;
male and female he created them"
(Genesis 1:27 ESV).

Everything that God does is infused with a divine purpose. God did not create anything that was insignificant. The crowning of his creation was man (men and women). My wife asked me what I thought the man's role was in marriage. I had to give it quite a bit of thought before I could answer that question. Here is what I came up with. Keep in mind that this is in no particular order, but it all applies.

Man up.

1 Corinthians 13:11 (NIV) says, "When I was a child, I talked like a child; I thought like a child, I reasoned like a child. When I became a man, I put the ways of childhood behind me."

God made us in his image. Since we are made in his image, the first task is to embrace manhood. What does it mean to be a man? Man up! It is time for men to act like men. I know that statement seems simple, but it is packed with truth. There are certain things that men must do. When you become a man, your focus is much different from when you were a child.

Men must focus on finding and fulfilling their God ordained purpose. The pursuit of a career, building a business, or completing their education to maximize potential. Men must pursue their purpose with passion and a relentless focus and recognize that failure is not an option. One of my mentors told me, "When you are in pursuit of your purpose, sleep becomes an interruption." Now, that is an example of a man in pursuit of his purpose. A man without a purpose is like a submarine with a screen door… useless. Purpose will drive you to achieve and reach your goal. Having a purpose will cause you to keep focus when everyone else around you is unfocused.

Husband.

Genesis 2:18 (NIV) says, "The Lord God said, 'It is not good for the man to be alone. I will make a helper suitable for him.'" God said it is not good for the man to be alone. He did not say it is not good for the boy to be alone. He said *man*. Getting to the stage of *man* is a process. I say this because boys use this stage as an excuse not to take responsibility. They say, "I'm still trying to get my life together, or once I make this amount of money or buy a house, that's when I can get married and settle down." Don't let the becoming a man stage progress forever. Because you were born male does not make you a man. You have to at some point know what direction you want to go in, whether it be a career, business, or education, as I already said.

Then, it is time to become a husband. I know that will not be popular with some men, but I believe that this is God's divine order. God said that he would make a helper suitable for man. He said a helper, not a second-class citizen but an equal. Someone like him. God didn't say he would give you helper(s), the word was singular one helper. I thank God daily for creating my wife for me.

A husband is responsible for the love in our marriages. (I hear crickets so I will repeat it.) The husband is responsible for the love in our marriages. We are to love our wife as Christ loved the church and gave himself up for her.

I know that TV shows, movies, and music glamorize the playboy lifestyle. I get it. I thought I was a player too. When my wife and I reacquainted, I was wearing playboy boots. (Don't laugh. I must've looked good. I got the girl.) But at some point, we have to retire our player card.

Stop making being a husband sound like you are going up for a life bid in the worst prison in the world. It's not a horrible thing. Having someone in your corner who truly has your back is worth millions.

Father.

Proverbs 1:8 (NIV) says, "Listen, my son, to your father's instruction and do not forsake your mother's teaching." There is a reason that God desires us to become men first, then husbands, and then fathers. It takes the first two stages to prepare you for fatherhood. Being a father is an extremely important job. In my role in the past as a pastor, I have counseled adult men that did not have a relationship with their fathers, and they were still carrying around the hurt and disappointment from an absent father. I have also counseled adult women who had an absent father, and they had a difficult time having a successful relationship because of the damage from an absent father or one that did not participate in their lives.

As fathers, we have a responsibility to love, honor, cherish, and protect our families. We can't decide that we want to see how many women we can play at once while making babies and leaving children without the presence of a father in their lives. Boys play those games. Men build families that are strong and meaningful. I understand that there are times when parents' divorce and go their separate ways for a number of reasons. This is no excuse for a man to divorce his children. We have responsibilities as fathers. Don't ever think that you have nothing to offer just because your own father was not there for you. That's a cop-out. Think about how you felt. Is that the way you want your child to feel? If your child is important to you, find a way to be a part of their lives. Men, we have responsibilities: we are responsible for teaching our sons how to treat women and for modeling the behavior that a man should have to our daughters.

Our children need us; they need us to be the man in their lives. They need us to model the unconditional love that God told us to have toward our wives and our children. When we stand up and take our rightful place, God is pleased, and divine order is intact in our families. The love bond becomes unbreakable, and we build boys into men and girls into women.

Show leadership.

First Corinthians 11:3 (NLT) says, "But there is one thing I want you to know: The head of every man is Christ, the head of woman is man, and the head of Christ is God." Being a leader does not mean that you rule with an iron fist. If you lead that way, you may end up just leading yourself. In the last few years, society has redefined the man's responsibilities in the family. There is a lack of good male role models in the home. Women are accepting the excuse that because he did not grow up with a father, it's OK that he does not know how to be a man and lead. You don't have to have a father in your home; some things can be learned just by surrounding yourself with good mentors. As the man of your home, show leadership, not dominance. You can't lead if you don't know where you are going. When your wife feels you can lead the family, she will have no problem following.

Love your wife unconditionally.

First Corinthians 13:4-7 (NLT) states

Love is patient and kind. Love is not jealous or boastful or proud or rude. It does not demand its own way. It is not irritable, and it keeps no record of being wronged. It does not rejoice about injustice but rejoices whenever the truth wins out. Love never gives up, never loses faith, is always hopeful, and endures through every circumstance."

To love your wife unconditionally is an act of will. You have to make a decision that you will love her through the barriers she puts up. Oh, I didn't mention that she will put up barriers? All of us bring our prior experiences into marriage. There are things that have happened in the past that will cause her to put up barriers.

When you love someone unconditionally, you patiently love them through those barriers.

To put it another way, loving someone unconditionally is loving them until they decide to let down their barriers because you have created an environment where they feel safe and comfortable enough to do so. Love her when she in a good mood or bad mood. Love her when she gains weight, when she is too skinny, or when she makes a mistake. Love her. Just like with everything else, there is a condition to unconditional love. Remember, not everyone deserves it.

We don't have to fix it.

I still struggle with this one. Most men want to solve or fix the problem. When my wife tells me something is bothering her, my brain goes into overdrive. I try to think of every scenario to fix her problem. We have grown to a point where she now says to me don't try to fix it, just listen. She could have saved me a whole lot of brain cells had she said that to me earlier in our marriage. There are times when our wives just want us to listen to what is on their hearts. Guys, we don't always have to fix it. Just be there to listen. It is important that we hear and address the concerns that are on our wives' hearts and minds. This will add to the intimacy of your marriage. Invest the necessary time to learn to understand what your wife needs. It is not always about the financial even though that is important. Men, we must spend time investing in the emotional well-being of our wives. This allows us to connect on another level.

Be her rock.

Matthew 16:18 (NLT) says, "Now I say to you that you are Peter (which means 'rock'), and upon this rock I will build my church, and all the powers of hell will not conquer it." Being your wife's rock means being a constant in her life a stabilizing force that she comes to depend on. You must be stable, reliable, and trustworthy. Additionally, be supportive and make her feel protected. Part of our responsibility as a husband is to make sure that our wives and families feel safe. We need to be reliable and dependable. I was always taught that my word is my bond. I still believe that. When my children were small, they caught on to this very quickly. If they asked me to take them somewhere and I said let me think about it, they considered this a no. Then they would ask, "Dad, do you promise?" Once I said I promised, they were confident that it would happen. Our wives expect us to be reliable and consistent. It seems like a no-brainer, but I will say it, anyway. Do what you are supposed to do. Be where you are supposed to be. Be a man of your word so that you are known to be a man of your word.

A provider.

Although it is very important to be a good financial provider, it is not the only support we need to provide to our wives. As the man, our role is to also provide emotional, spiritual, and physical support. For most men, that is not something that comes naturally. However, this does not give us an excuse. We can learn anything that we put our minds to. As long as we have the desire and motivation, we can do it.

A teacher.

Men, let's teach our sons to be men and our daughters to be ladies. Be a teacher to our wives and learn from her as well. Teach love, respect, and work ethics, and be the example of what you teach. Find out what your wife is interested in. You should know her hopes and dreams and push her to reach them.

The protector.

Protect her, even if you have to sacrifice yourself. Your role as the man is to protect your family. My wife always makes the joke that we should do the Bonnie and Clyde thing and rob banks. I always tell her, "Heck no! I'm not robbing no banks with you. You can't even run." I would have to sacrifice myself so that she could get away. That's funny but that's the man's role. We have to physically protect her, protect her self-esteem, her love, and her heart. We also have to protect her reputation. I must admit, when I am with a group of men and I hear a man tearing down his wife and talking about her shortcomings and how she is just a mess, I immediately think that this is a man that I cannot trust. If he will say things about his wife, then I don't stand a chance at him having my back. Now, I am not saying that my wife is perfect far from it. As her protector, it is my job to help build her up, encourage her, and protect her name and reputation at all times. She represents you, and you represent her. Operate as a team.

The listener.
I had to end this chapter with this very important quality of a man. Be a good listener. Men, listen to your wives; they are smart about a lot of subjects. I believe God gave women a special kind of discerning ability. Anytime I want to do business with a person, I let them meet my wife. Once she has a conversation with the person, I don't know what kind of feeling she gets. But if she says, "Babe, I don't think we should do business with this person," I usually won't. She has not been wrong yet. Ask your wife her opinion on things that concern you, take the time to listen to her opinion, and value what she has to say. You don't have to ask the opinions of your parents, siblings, and friends. Listen to what your woman has to say; you'll be blessed. I always know that my wife has my best interest at heart. Why wouldn't she? We are one. We are on the same team, and our goals, hopes, and dreams are in alignment. Why wouldn't I listen to her? It does not make me soft or weak because I listen to my wife. I value her counsel, ideas, intellect, and spiritual guidance.

Men, we need to take our place and handle our

responsibilities. We must man up and operate in a way that our wife, children, and community will respect. I could go on, but that would be another book. I'm not trying to give her any ideas . . .

Chapter 15

FOR THE LOVE OF MONEY

A Financial Groove

Ramona Jones

"Have You Prayed Together Today?"

"For the love of money is the root of all kinds of evil. And some people, craving money, have wandered from the true faith and pierced themselves with many sorrows" (1 Timothy 6:10 NIV).

People often say that the Bible says that money is the root of all evil. It clearly does not say that. The scripture says that the love of money is the root of all evil (1 Timothy 6:10). Money matters. We need money. It's the currency that helps us to operate our everyday lives. It's a necessity. Even the most frugal person in the world still needs that all mighty dollar in order to operate.

The Bible never told us not to make money. In fact, it says if you don't work you shouldn't eat. Suffice to say, in order to eat, you have to make money, and in order to make money, you have to work. It's a vicious cycle, but such is life.

When you enter into a marriage, the topic of finances, money, dollar bills, cash, paper, greenbacks, cheddar, or whatever you choose to call it, must be discussed.

We need to understand the differences in how our partner handles their finances versus the way we handle ours. It can become very problematic to enter a relationship with someone who has insurmountable debt that occurred before you married.

This may not be popular, but before we marry, we should look at each other's credit reports. We need to know what kind of debt we are marrying into. Although this debt may have occurred before you married and your spouse may never ask you for any help with paying it, you must consider how your spouse using part of their income on past debt will affect your lifestyle together.

Ask your spouse about things like alimony, child support, late taxes, student loans, etc. Don't let a wage garnishment be the reason you find out that your spouse is eighteen years behind on child support. Never just assume that finances are OK. Just because your partner has a master's or a doctorate degree and a great career does not mean that they are not one paycheck away from bankruptcy.

Ask yourself if you are really ready to enter into a relationship with ready-made debt. Are you willing to use what should be your play money or savings to help clear up debt your partner incurred before the two of you married and potentially debt that they made with an ex?

When my husband and I married, we were both just starting to establish credit, so the debt we created, we created together. However, we did have to get used to each other's spending habits. My husband was in the military before we married, therefore, he had three hot's and a cot (three meals and a bed) daily, and whatever money he earned, he was free to spend it as he pleased.

I, on the other hand, was a single mother with rent to pay, childcare, food, bills, etc. I have always lived by a budget which made our differences in spending money a topic of conversation on a lot of nights. In the early years of our marriage, if my husband saw something he wanted, he bought it. Granted, sometimes, it would be a bouquet of roses or a piece of jewelry for me. Still, in the back of my mind, I would calculate how much he'd just used from our already tight budget. (It may seem I was being ungrateful, but do you know how much a dozen roses cost?)

Never assume money matters will just work themselves out because they never will. As a couple, you will need to decide if you will have separate accounts, joint accounts, or both. Discuss if both of you will work outside of the home. Also, when you decide to have children, will one of you stay home to care for the children, or will there be childcare?

Discuss who will be in charge of paying the monthly bills. (Please understand that we are not all good in the department of paying bills.) Come to an agreement on who will pay each bill and stick to it. No one likes to walk into their home and the lights are off. Now, you are looking at each other saying, "I thought you were going to pay that bill."

I call our home DJMona Inc. I have been the CFO of DJMona Inc. for over thirty years. It is a well-run organization and has held strong over the decades. I work other jobs outside of DJMona Inc. over the years, but no other company is more important to me than our company. I run our corporation with a fine-tooth comb. I keep it well organized, the bills are paid on time, and things don't get cut off because I mismanaged the company's funds. In our corporation, we don't make large spending decisions without consulting the board. The board consists of DJ and Mona. And most importantly, we pay ourselves.

I do realize that a lot of couples keep their finances completely separate. The husband pays his half of the house note, the wife hers. She pays the cable and trash, and he gets the lights and the gas. They go half on the food and other expenditures. He doesn't know her salary, and she doesn't know his. As long as each person can pay their half of the expenses, it's all good.

If that works for your marriage, it's all good. But for me, if I had wanted a roommate, I had girlfriends for that. Some marriages come across as roommates who are only together to share expenses. I read a post on social media that said, "Real men provide. Real women appreciate it." I didn't see anything wrong with the post. But apparently, some women were outraged.

Women were saying, "Why should I have to sit back and appreciate a man for providing for me? I can provide for myself." I'm sure that the post was not implying that men are the only ones who provide. We are aware that women provide and are sometimes the main breadwinner in the household. But if your man is providing, then why shouldn't you appreciate him?

I'm an old school girl, and I married an old school guy.

When we dated, he paid for our dates. I didn't rush to put my credit card down to show him that I was independent and could afford to buy my own meal, although, when we first got married, I was making a higher salary than he was.

In the early years of being married, I have worked inside the home. When I did take a job outside, it was contract work. This is OK for the Jones's because we talked about this during the course of our marriage.

I have a sister-in-law who, whenever I told her I was working one of my contract jobs, would call me Rochelle. She would say, "Rochelle, how long are going to be on that job?" Rochelle is the name of a sitcom character from a show called *Everybody Hates Chris*. My sister-in-law would always say to me "You don't need that job, Mona; your man got two jobs."

I finally had to take the time and actually watch this show. Rochelle and her husband Julius were what I consider an old school couple. The husband worked more than one job, and the wife worked outside of the home, sometimes, or when things got tight. When the job got to be too stressful or she didn't want to work outside the home anymore, she would quit. (Her catch phrase was, "I ain't got to take this. My husband got two jobs.")

This sitcom portrayed a man that was holding it down for his family. Yes, he did have to work more than one job sometimes. But while he was working his job, she ran the cooperation at home and managed the children.

Some men will never take care of their woman like Rochelle's husband did, and some women will never depend on a man to do so. But come on, ladies. You have to admit, sometimes, it feels good for your man to say, "Baby, I got you."

Make it a priority to discuss finances. Don't let the love of money be the thing that destroys your marriage. Money does matter.

During the course of our marriage, we discussed financial goals. One of my husband's goals was to start a business. Darryl has worked in corporate sales for the majority of his adult life.

He saw an opportunity we discussed it, prayed about it, and he went for it. He went to the owner of the company that he was working for and told him that he would like to become an independent contractor. He wanted to maintain the current clients that he had, but instead of being an employee, he would be an independent contractor. The owner agreed, and this was the beginning of Jones' Sales Solutions. We were a project management firm that provided consultation, move management, and project management for corporations that needed to move their businesses. One of the first contracts that DJ landed was a million-dollar account. It was exciting and scary at the same time. He needed to hire a project manager right away. He came home the night after signing contracts and told me, "I have a great idea, babe. I want you to take the position for our company as a project manager.

I told him that I did not have experience in project managing. He gave me the look that only he can give me. "Of course, you do! You have been running DJMona corporation for years. You handle the bills, keep the schedule for the kids, and keep my schedule. You make sure all the pieces move in the right place. Project managing is the same thing. You keep a timeline and manage the steps of the relocation."

I took the position. I must tell you, it was some of the most challenging work that I have ever done, and I absolutely loved it. We were able to build a business together. He worked during the day, selling and obtaining new clients. I worked midday to late night, project managing the relocations. We ended up with a total of four project managers in our business. There is no limit to what two people that love each other and God can accomplish. When we love each other, we are able to find our financial groove.

Chapter 16

FOR MY KING, MY MAN

A Kings Groove

Ramona Jones

"Have You Prayed Together Today?"

"The king is lying on his couch, enchanted by the fragrance of my perfume" (Song of Solomon 1:12 NLT).

What is a man? Webster defines a man as a noun: an adult male human being. A man or boy who shows the qualities (such as strength and courage) that men are traditionally supposed to have.

Infinity is the word that comes to mind when I think of a word to describe a man. There are so many different ways to define a man the answers can go on forever. I hear women say that they are looking for a good man, for their king. Are you really ready for a king? There is nothing wrong with wanting a king. My husband is my rock; he is my king, and I treat him as such. Treating him like a king doesn't make me a servant, but serving each other is something couples should do.

According to 1 Peter 4:10 (ESV), "As each has received a gift, use it to serve one another, as good stewards of God's varied grace." Some would say I'm lucky to have the marriage that I have. I say I'm just blessed. I don't just have a good man: I have a God man. He loves God first, then me. Most women want to be treated like a queen. That's the new thing I hear a lot of people saying. He's my king, and she's my queen. But if you know anything about kings and queens, they are catered to. They are treated well and respected. You can't use that verbiage and not understand what a king and queen are. It's more than having high incomes, thinking we can be a power couple. It's so much more than that. You can have the money, wealth, and the material things, but if you are not on one accord, all that won't even matter. You have to set some sort of standards in your marriage. Ladies, when you make the decision to call a man your king, understand that there is some servitude involved.

I serve my king because he's worthy. Only you know if your king is worthy. I can give you a list of things that make a man king worthy, but that would be my list. We all have different things that make our king worthy to us. In the grand scheme of things, we are the only ones who have the final vote. Like I said earlier, the qualities that define a man are infinite.

MY KING:

Make your king feel sexy.

When my husband looks good, I make sure I tell him "Honey, you looking good today. My Sexual Chocolate."

When he puts on cologne, I tell him he smells good, even though I'm allergic to almost all perfumes and colognes. I still love it when he wears cologne.

When he gets a fresh haircut and shave, I notice. I love it when my husband notices that I have done something different to my hair, or I have a fresh new style. Well, when he gets a fresh cut, style, or twist, notice him.

Make sure your king knows you need him.

Women make our own money; we can have and rear children with or without a man, we can take our own cars to be serviced, and buy our own homes. But our Kings still need to feel that they are needed. Yeah, you can lift weights at the gym, but at home, ask him to move the sofa for you. Allow him to open the door for you and pay the check when you go out. Ask his opinion about important decisions. Make sure he knows you need him.

Fix your king's plate.

Yeah, I know this is old school. I already told ya'll this is an old school groove. Of course, he can fix his own plate. But it's OK to serve your king, sometimes. Whether you are at home or visiting friends and family, serve your man his plate; it makes him feel special. Serve it with love. You know what your man likes to eat. Don't just slop something on his plate and give it to him. Prepare it with love.

Be available.

When I say be available, I'm not saying be at his beck and call because who has time for that? When he needs to talk to you, if at all possible, be available. Pay attention to him, make eye contact, ask questions, and show interest.

Don't lose your sexy.

Men are very visual creatures. You dress up for work, and you dress up when you are going out with the girls. Why not dress up for your king? If the two of you go out to lunch or brunch on the weekends, don't just throw on your yoga pants with no makeup and pull your hair in a bun. (I'm guilty of this look.) Look good for your king; dress it up a little. Make your king feel proud that he is with you. Ladies, keep it sexy in the bedroom for your king; surprise him by having him come home to Vixen Vicky or Tantalizing Tammy instead of Frumpy Fanny or Sloppy Sally. If you have lost your sexy, it's time to go find her and bring her back.

Make his home his castle.

Make your household a place of peace. Keep it drama free. Don't let your friends and family bring their drama to your home. Don't get caught up in someone else's drama. Just because your friend's man is cheating on her doesn't mean your man is cheating on you. Just because your friends' kids are out of control doesn't mean all children are out of control.

Show your intellect.

It's OK to show him and his friends that he married you for more than just your looks and hot body.

Encourage him.

Tell your husband you appreciate him and all he does for your family. Let him know you respect and value him. Encourage him when he wants to go for that promotion or start a business. Know when he needs to talk or when he just needs to think things out on his own.

Watch out for his health.

Make sure your man goes to the doctor and gets regular checkups. Schedule the appointments yourself if you have to. Don't say he's a grown man; he should go to the doctor. Most men don't go unless something is really wrong. Pay attention when he starts new medications and read up on the side effects.

Pray for him.

Pray for your king. Pray that he continues to keep his relationship with God first. Pray for his health and for his career. Pray that God continues to give him the wisdom to lead your family.

Chapter 17

MY QUEEN, MY WOMAN

A Queen's Groove

Darryl (DJ) Jones

"Have You Prayed Together Today?"

"How beautiful are your sandaled feet,
O queenly maiden.
Your rounded thighs are like jewels,
the work of a skilled craftsman" (Song of
Solomon 7:1 NLT).

You don't have to be like the guy on the movie *Coming to America* and sing "She's Your Queen." But it is our job as her man to make her feel like a queen.

Tell your queen she's beautiful.

I always tell my wife that she is beautiful because it is the truth, from her sexy walk to the way that she looks at me across a room. That knowing glance that I give her that says to her subliminally, "Babe, you still got it." Whenever, and I do mean whenever, she passes by, I feel a need to touch her or smack her on the bottom. I want her to always know that I see her and that I think she is as beautiful and sexy as the day I first met her.

Yes, it's OK if she enhances her beauty with makeup, hairstyles, and fashion. But with every other commercial talking about makeup, diet pills, and weight loss surgery, it's nice for her to hear that I think she's beautiful just the way she is.

Be her protector.

I have this running joke with my wife. I tell her often that I allow her to stay in her bubble. In her bubble, she has no concerns, and things are just fine. Outside of that bubble, when I enter a room (part of this is from military training) I will never sit with my back to the door. I am looking for exits and for who is standing between us and the nearest exit in case something happens while we are there. I am sizing up any potential threat and planning a strategy to neutralize that threat in the most efficient way. All this is going on in my mind while babe is enjoying our conversation over a candlelit dinner. She is in her bubble while I am planning. When we are walking in public together, I will not allow anyone that I don't know to get closer than three feet. If they try to, I will stop her from walking and approach them and find out what is going on. It is much more than just physical protection; Always protect your queen. Protect her physically, mentally, and spiritually. Don't allow anyone to make your queen feel scared or afraid. Be her protector; be her hero hence her bubble of safety.

Brag about your queen.

My wife is one of the most driven people that I know. She decided she wanted to be an author, so what did she do? She wrote three books! Who does that? Wife, mother, entrepreneur, counselor, advisor, and all-around dynamic, phenomenal woman. There is no one like babe. Never be jealous of your spouse's accomplishments. It's OK to brag about your queen's accomplishments to others. Let the world know how proud you are.

Give her your attention.

When you love someone, I believe that it is a sign of love and respect when you give them your undivided attention. I know that I am able to do quite a bit of multitasking, and I am pretty accomplished at it. However, when babe needs to talk to me, I turn off the TV, put the iPad and iPhone down, and turn off the computer. (Yes, I pretty much have a control center going when I am multitasking.) I want her to always feel that she is my priority. The other things that I am working on can wait when she needs to talk to me. I never want her to feel that any of the other things I am working on are more important than she is. Time is the one thing that we can't get back. So, when I invest time in her, it is always a great investment. Babe has my full attention when she needs it.

Have mind-blowing sex.

Giving and receiving. In my mind, this is what mind-blowing sex is comprised of. If you are focused on pleasing, your wife will reciprocate. Never be selfish with your queen. Take care of yourself physically. Nobody, and I mean nobody, wants "end of the day, tired, exhausted sex." Make a plan. Take an afternoon off, buy her favorite bubble bath, flowers, and candles. Set the mood. I know if I go home early, clean the house, wash dishes, mop, and vacuum, my wife is already excited. Sometimes, it is alright to have sports car sex. Other times, you want the sustained limo ride sex. Both have their place and time. Don't be selfish when it comes to sex. Make love to your queen; take time to enjoy her.

Treat her how she wants to be treated.

I was reared by my parents to be a gentleman. I believe in opening doors and giving my seat when a lady enters the room. Once, I was at a trade show, and in the booth across from me, I saw a lady trying to move a heavy trunk. There were three men in the booth, and they did not offer her any assistance. I headed over to the booth and asked the guys, "Why aren't you helping the lady?"

She looked at me and said, "I am not a lady. I am a woman." *What?* I was floored. I had no words. When I got home, I had to ask my wife about this. What does it mean? My wife said maybe she wanted to be treated equal to the guys, or maybe she has never been treated like a lady before. Either way, it did not make sense to me. When I am assisting a lady, I am doing so, not because I think she is not capable or able to do for herself, I'm doing it because I am a gentleman. I always treat my wife as a lady. And when any other lady is in my presence, I treat them the same way. Our wives want to be treated like a lady, a queen. Always treat her with love and, most of all, respect.

Be someone she can depend on.

It is important to be dependable and consistent. If you say you are going to take care of it, then do it. If you say you got it, then have it. If you say you're going to be there, then be there. If you say you're going to do something, then do it. She shouldn't have to worry because you have shown her, she can depend on you.

Trust her opinion.

I have always trusted my wife's opinion. As I have mentioned before, she has the gift of discernment. When you trust someone's opinion, it does not mean that you agree with everything they have to say, but it does mean that you value their input when you are making decisions that will affect you both. Listen to her, and address her concerns. It could save you from a lot of trouble later on. Ask your wife her opinion on subjects that concern you. Listen to her and trust that what she says has your best interests in mind.

Encourage her.

Part of our job as a husband is to be a people builder. It is so easy to tear down and destroy. Spend your time encouraging and pushing your wife. Let her know that you believe in her and her dreams. Be the catalyst that pushes her over the top on her goal. And not with just lip service. Invest in her development. Sometimes, we all need that little push. Encourage your queen. See her potential, and encourage her to reach her highest high.

Pray for her.

You are the covering for your wife. Don't let the day end or let her leave home without a prayer of covering. Pray for strength, peace, and health. Pray that God will use every gift and ability that He has placed inside of her. Pray that she has the confidence to take on any and all challenges that will come her way. Pray that her hopes, dreams, and visions come to pass. Never let her go out uncovered without God's protection. Always pray for your queen.

The king and queen are two separate individuals. They are independent of each other, but when they come together, they can accomplish so much more than they could independently.

Chapter 18

MARRIAGE AND MENOPAUSE

A Body Change Groove

Ramona Jones

"Have You Prayed Together Today?"

"And now, in my old age, don't set me aside. Don't forsake me now when my strength is failing" (Psalm 71:9NLT).

This may be the realist chapters in the book. And it is needed; we try to skip around this very odd, stressful change in marriage. But it's something we can't ignore. This change can destroy a marriage if not approached correctly. It's called menopause, or "the change."

According to the Oxford's English Dictionary, menopause is the ceasing of menstruation. The period in a woman's life (typically between forty-five and fifty years of age) when this occurs.

When we look up the word menopause, we get the above definition. When I was younger, I used to think to myself, *What woman would not look forward to having no monthly period? No more cramps, no more bloating, no more chocolate or salt cravings, and all the other symptoms that come with this time of the month.* Gurl, somebody should have told me.

The ceasing of menstruation is the only good thing that we get from this change in life. I had no idea that there were so many other symptoms associated with menopause. I had to write this chapter about menopause because there are so many women going through this change in life and don't know how to handle it. And to make an already difficult situation worse, our men don't know how to handle this life change, either. Now, I really understand why they call it, "the change." Menopause is a complete life-changing experience. A woman's body starts to go through another blossoming. We blossom from girl to woman. Then, we blossom from woman to wisdom.

OK, let's explore the menopause life. Whatever stage you are in perimenopause or menopause, women don't feel like themselves. We are trying to control our out-of-control hormones. We are trying to get ahold of our body changes. Guys, remember this is new for us, too. We understand you are watching your wife change right before your eyes. But she is trying to get a grip on the change that is happing right before her own eyes as well. Come with me; let's take a small look at life with menopause.

There is an increase in midsection fat.

I'm a thick girl, and I dig that about myself. But somebody is not playing fair. Because someone put a nonremovable inner tube around my midsection while I was sleeping and won't take it back.

According to Healthline.com, menopause can also include hormone fluctuations. Both elevated and very low levels of estrogen can lead to increased fat storage. Fat is hard to lose, but not impossible.

Insomnia might occur.

I was that girl who took naps on the weekends and was still able to go to sleep at bedtime. When menopause entered my world, I was lucky if I got three to four hours for the whole day. Usually, my husband and I go to bed around ten or eleven o'clock. But menopause had me awake sometimes until six the next morning.

According to Healthline.com, "During perimenopause (and menopause), your ovaries begin producing lower amounts of key hormones. This includes estrogen and progesterone. As these hormone levels fall, symptoms of menopause surge. One such symptom is insomnia."

You might experience body aches.

I don't even know when I started groaning when I stood up. And when did my muscles start feeling like I'm doing a powerlifting workout daily?

According to Kathryn M Landherr MD, Board Certified

ObGyn in a blog on menopause and chronic pain dated Nov 13, 2015, "There are various types of pain and discomfort associated with menopause. The most common are the result of chronic inflammation such as bone, joint, and muscle aches… As the body's production of hormones changes during menopause, the loss of estrogen can cause inflammation."

Fatigue might be common.

I am usually a pretty active person. My husband and I work out at the gym, go for walks on the beach, and I'm always down to go somewhere when asked. When menopause entered my world, just the thought of going to the gym or walking made me tired. My best friend was the couch; I felt tired all the time. Remember, I told y'all I was barely getting any sleep, so I was always fatigued.

According to Healthline.com, "The same hormonal changes that cause symptoms like hot flashes and night sweats can also affect your mood and energy levels, leading to fatigue. Those hormone variations can also make it harder for you to sleep at night, which can leave you feeling tired during the day."

It might cause hair loss.

Now, this one really ticked me off. I have locs in my hair; suddenly, they began to get super thin and break, and my eyebrows started thinning. So now, I have thinning hair and no eyebrows. *Gurl*, that ain't sexy.

According to Healthline.com, "Research suggests that hair loss during menopause is the result of a hormonal imbalance. Specifically, it's related to a lowered production of estrogen and progesterone."

You might develop anxiety and depression.

This is not one of the symptoms that I dealt, although

sometimes, I did feel a little down. But I have talked to women who feel anxiety and depression daily.

According to Clevelandclinic.org, "The fluctuation of estrogen and another key hormone, progesterone, in your body can cause feelings of anxiety or depression. But frequent, troubling high anxiety or panic attacks are not a normal part of menopause. Some women develop a panic disorder during menopause (and even panic attacks)."

Low or no sex drive and vaginal dryness might develop.

Ladies, believe me when I say I didn't see this one coming. Mr. Affectionate was really thrown off by this one. When you have a healthy and enjoyable sex life that goes from one hundred to zero, you have to wonder what the hell is going on. Not only does the body lose the desire to make love, but it also loses the intimate sensations. My husband could just touch my neck and send a sensation throughout my body. It all ended with menopause. Now remember, I already told y'all my husband is a very affectionate man. He had a very difficult time not sleeping snuggled up next to me. He also struggled with me not having desire for him. (Sorry; way too hot for that.)

According to Healthline.com, "Menopause can negatively affect libido in several ways. During menopause, your testosterone and estrogen levels both decrease, which may make it more difficult for you to get aroused. A decrease in estrogen can also lead to vaginal dryness. Lower levels of estrogen lead to a drop-in blood supply in the vagina, which can then negatively affect vaginal lubrication. It can also lead to thinning of the vaginal wall, known as vaginal atrophy. Vaginal dryness and atrophy often lead to discomfort during sex.

Hold on don't panic ladies. I have good news, trouble don't last always. For most of us, the desire does come back. (Thank you, Lord. I was in that number!) And they're plenty of over-the-counter products for dryness.

There might be both moodiness and irritability.

There are so many things that can make you grumpy and irritable during menopause. For starters, having hot flashes and not being able to sleep. Another is trying to put on a pair of jeans and you're bloated. Your hormonal balance is off, and so is your personality. I would tell my husband sometimes, "I'm in a mood today."

He'd say to me, "Take you and your mood in the other room, or go take a bath." I didn't want to take my bad mood out on him, and believe me, he didn't want me to. And I thank God that he didn't get angry with me for being moody.

You might have hot flashes and night sweats.

The only way I can describe a hot flash is to say your body feels like a volcano that is going to erupt. The heat starts to simmer in your toes, then it rises through your whole body like hot lava. It erupts from your body in a flush or night sweat. I was never much of a sweater. Even when I exercised, I would do a sexy perspire. But now, when I attempt to exercise, I don't know who that hard breathing, sweaty monster is. And the night sweats are not a normal kind of sweat. You are sleeping. No activity just sleep. And heat wakes you up from a sound sleep, gripping your whole body like a flame.

When I first started having hot flashes, it was horrible. I would say to myself, *This is not of God. God must be allowing the devil to punish me for past sins and sins to come.* I remember thinking *I just can't believe that another woman has gone through this and didn't make a public service announcement, a movie of the week, or something.* I said to myself, *I must be the only one with overactive symptoms of menopause. Where is Oprah when we need her?* Gurl, I needed a show about this.

My poor husband must have thought I was losing my mind. I would have the air on full blast and sleep on top of the covers. Or have the window open and the fan turned on. He saw how much I was suffering one night, so he put ice in an ice chest, along with a towel; so that I could grab the towel to cool off when I had a flash. (Love me some him)

According to Healthline.com, "Menopausal hot flashes are sudden feelings of intense body heat that can occur during the day or night. Night sweats are periods of heavy sweating, or hyperhidrosis, associated with hot flashes that occur at night. ... They're your body's reactions to the hormonal changes associated with peri-menopause and menopause."

You might have migraines.

I once worked with a lady who experienced migraines all the time. Sometimes, she would still manage to come to work when they were mild, but she would always wear dark shades. I remember asking her, "Are the headaches that bad?" Now, I understand. Your head is throbbing, and no over-the-counter painkiller can make it go away. When the light hits your eyes, they feel like they are bleeding. I had my first migraine when I first entered the world of menopause. I took Tylenol, prescription strength Motrin, and a few other things. Nothing helped, so I just lie in my dark bedroom with a towel on my eyes, praying the pain away. The pain is horrible, and I feel for the people who suffer with migraines on a regular basis.

According to menopause.org, "Menopause may make migraines less severe if they were linked to the hormonal fluctuations of menstrual cycle. Or migraines may start for the first time, or worsen, around perimenopause because of new hormonal fluctuations."

You might experience brain fog.

This one really scared me. I remember thinking I was experiencing early onset Alzheimer's, the way I would forget things. I mean, someone would have a whole conversation with me, and I wouldn't remember sometimes. Or I would be in mid-sentence and could not remember the word I wanted to use. (I now call it my "tip of the tongue" syndrome.) I also had to walk away from a job because I couldn't comprehend the training. I have never had problems learning new things, but the training felt like they were doing it in a foreign language. It was a crazy experience.

If you are married, it is imperative that you talk to your husband about what's happening with your body. We have to do the research, and then research some more, and did I say research? I did so much research on menopause that I could fill up an entire room. I could barely get a grip on what was going on with my own body. How could I expect my husband to understand? When it comes to combating menopausal symptoms, one size does not fit all. Do your research, and make an informative decision for what's best for you. There are so many different things we can try to alleviate the symptoms from herbal remedies like maca, primrose, black cohosh, apple cider vinegar, etc. Believe me, I know. I have a menopause medicine cabinet. Or we can try hormone replacement therapy, or Bioidentical Hormone Replacement Therapy. Don't go by what someone tells you their experience was. Hormone replacement therapy may be just what you need to get that reboot. Do what's best for you. Don't let menopause make you give up on your marriage; this is one of those twists and turns down that bumpy road called marriage. It won't last always.

On a side note, something we don't hear about, but I truly believe men go through *manipause*. Yeah, I know it's not a real thing, but I think it should be. It's not a midlife crisis they are going through, it's *manipause*. They get the midsection spread that's hard to get rid of. They have trouble getting muscle gain like they used to. They start dying their hair and beards. They get a little cranky for no reason. Their sex drive is not like it used to be.

I have talked to married women who say their husbands are not as sexual as they used to be. I tell them if he has gone from a few times a week to one time a week, that's cool. Just make sure that it is not something physical that's causing this. Wives, we have to make sure we check all side effects to medication he is taking, watch his diet, and make sure he is getting some exercise. Things will be OK; we can work through anything together.

Chapter 19

GROWING OLD TOGETHER

An Aging Groove

Ramona Jones

"Have You Prayed Together Today?"

"They shall still bring forth fruit in old age; they shall be fat and flourishing" (Psalm 92:14 KJV).

I love to see older couples walking together and still holding hands. That is an example I see from my mother and father-in-law. They have been married for over sixty years. They do everything together, and it is not uncommon to see them holding hands.

I hope it's safe to say that some of us will actually grow old together. I hope when you enter into marriage, you enter believing you will grow old together. Growing old with the person you love is a blessing from God. This is the person who knows you and you know them. Every laugh line and wrinkle is beautiful to them. Every gray hair shows signs of your wisdom, and every extra roll is just a sexy love cushion.

I have been married for three decades. *Wow!* Sometimes, I still find that amazing, and I have to stop and thank God for giving me the man who was not perfect, but perfect for me.

When you age together, you will have some awesome stories to tell. We raised four children and now have six grandchildren. At this point in our lives, we can sit back and enjoy the fruits of our labor.

Marriage should be like fine wine. It's supposed to get better with time. I understand that yes, it can be an emotional roller coaster filled with different wants and needs, different fears, and insecurities, but it is a great accomplishment to be able to say we went through the storms and rains and made it. And guess what? We made it together.

In this chapter of the book, I will give you some reasons why it's great to grow old together.

In Proverbs 5:18 (KJV), it says, "Let thy fountain be blessed, and rejoice with the wife of thy youth." Men, the Bible tells you that your fountain will be blessed if you rejoice with the wife of your youth. It does not say that once she gets old and worn, to go get another wife so your fountain can continue to be blessed. It says rejoice in the wife of your youth. Love each other, cherish each other, and rejoice in each other.

The children have moved out.

Over the course of raising children, you may have said. "I will be glad when my children are grown and are on their own." And I'm sure your children may have said." I can't wait to move out on my own."

Well, we've made it. We have the empty nest, the children are grown, they are out of the house, and it's just the two of you, now. You don't have to worry about childcare anymore. You get to cook for two, or go out to have a meal for a party of two. You can downsize your residence. Why do you need three thousand square feet for two people?

You get to get rid of the mom car.

(This one was special for me.) I always drove minivans and SUV's. I'd dropped off kids to sport's events, malls, and friend's houses. When the children started to drive, they always drove my car. When I was younger, I would always wonder why older people would buy two-seater sports cars. Now, I understand. It's because you no longer have to buy a car according to how many children you have. I have always loved the Chevy Camaro, but with four children, that was not practical. Now, I'm going to be a sexy senior in my convertible Chevy Camaro with my sexy senior honey.

You know each other better than anyone else.

Aging together is such an awesome experience. This person knows you better than anyone else. Sometimes, better than you know yourself.

It's still funny to me when my husband and I go out for breakfast. I order my food, and I always forget to ask for salsa for my eggs. And then, I'm impatient when the server takes too long to bring it. Now, my husband always says, "Bring her salsa, please."

When you age together you get to know each other's idiosyncrasies. I know my husband is not good when it comes to sharing his electronics. He will only share his computer if he absolutely has to, never because he wants to. He keeps all the boxes for his small electronics. They are all in good condition and look like they did when he purchased them. If he passes them on to someone else, they will come with the original box, the plugs, and the instructions. (Unless I made the mistake of tossing them.)

You will experience changes.

When aging together, you will go through different transitions in life. Career changes, deaths of parents and love ones, midlife crises, and body changes. But you must still, love one another.

Receiving the blessings of becoming grandparents.

We are grandparents to six amazing little people. Being called Granny, GG, Papa, or Pau-Pau is our reward. We get to spoil our grandchildren and give them things that their parents have said no too. And the best part is we get to send them home. It's such a wonderful feeling to see the fruits of your loins and say we did that.

Experiencing great sex.

Great sex doesn't happen right away, it takes time. Some people think that when you get to a certain age, you shouldn't have sex. Well, I don't subscribe to that way of thinking. When you have grown old together, you know each other's bodies. There is no getting it wrong. Sex should only get better. If you want to scream out, it's OK. Nobody is home except you. He may have a bad back, and she may have bad knees. Work it out. Mature lovemaking is the best sex you can have. You take your time; there's no pressure.

You stop caring about what people think.

This one took me a little while, but as you get older you start saying, "I'm way too old for the madness, and I really don't care what you think." If you have agreed together as a couple that this is the way you are going to do something, you couldn't care less who agrees. My husband never had this problem; he couldn't care less about what someone thought when he made a decision. (And I dig that about him.)

You encourage each other to fulfill dreams that were put on hold.

Dreams get put on hold sometimes because of careers, children, and family just the vicissitudes of life. As you age together, encourage each other to follow some of those dreams that were put on hold. Those dreams are still a part of you. Go back to school, paint a picture, start a business, or like I did, write a book. Dust those dreams off and get to work. You'll be happy that you at least gave it a try. It's never too late to fulfill a dream.

Enjoy more time together.

You don't have to have a lot of people around all the time or go to parties. You can enjoy a quiet evening at home together. Binge-watch a TV show, play your mixed tape, and just talk. (Every couple should have their own mixed tape. The definition of a mixed tape is a mixture of love songs that make you think about how much you love your mate.) Honey and I love all music; sorry, but I can't get romantic and intimate with gospel music playing in the background. Y'all betta make a mixed tape; it will do wonders for your together time.

You have inside jokes and can act silly together.

Be silly together have fun. Just because you are older, don't take life so seriously all the time. My husband and I share tons of inside jokes. Sometimes, we have to tell each other "I'm not going to even look at you," because we know one of us is doing something silly. At any moment, we will burst out singing or dancing. We have fun. Laugh couples; it will add years to your life.

You get to give relationship advice to younger couples.

It's sometimes funny when I hear a single, young person giving marital advice to a young married couple. The problem is, that person has absolutely no idea what it is like to be married. Don't get me wrong, just because someone has been married for years does not make them an expert. We can only share what works for our individual relationships. The person receiving the advice has to take pieces from all the advice received and put together something that works for them.

CHAPTER 20

WE MADE IT:

WE ~~SURVIVED~~ THRIVED THE WHOLE GROOVE

A Final Groove

Darryl (DJ) Jones

"Have You Prayed Together Today?"

"But they that wait upon the Lord shall renew their strength; they shall mount up with wings as eagles; they shall run, and not be weary, and they shall walk, and not faint" (Isaiah 40:1 KJV).

We made it. We are still grooving together. We've hit some bumps, had some ups and downs, and made some wild turns, but we stayed the course. Nothing but smooth sailing from now on, right? Um, sorry to disappoint.

The truth is, marriage is an ongoing process where the education never ends. There may always be bumps or curves, but if you stay in your own lane and learn how to maneuver a little better, your marriage will make it to the final groove. The secret to a long-lasting happy marriage is… There are no secrets! Each marriage has its own individual challenges. We can't compare our marriages to others and ask why our partners don't act like him or her. You are not him or her; you are you. What one person may be able to tolerate for years, another person won't deal with it for a week.

Our goal should be to make our own marriage the best marriage it can be. Not saying that we shouldn't have role models, just don't try to make your spouse into someone else.

All in all, love and marriage are not such bad things. Growing old together is beautiful. It's not something people used to do. Strong, loving marriages are something people still do. But you have to be willing to do the work.

Good marriages don't just happen. It takes two people who are willing to build each other up instead of tearing each other down. You have to support each other spiritually, financially, emotionally, physically. And every other supportive way. Marriage is ride or die. But ride or die has to be a two-way street. We have to be willing to ride or die for each other. We must have each other's backs. No one should come between our marital bond.

Mark 10:9 says, ". . .What therefore God hath joined together, let not man put asunder." (Which simply means don't let anyone separate you.)

Remember, a groove is an established routine or habit. Staying together requires us to find our groove. That is the exciting part of marriage to me. Getting to know her and finding out what she likes and dislikes what makes her happy. It still amazes me that my wife is happy if I clean the kitchen and the bathroom. I know its kind of random, but let me explain. Since I am from a military background, when I clean the bathroom, I am not satisfied until all the chrome is polished and shining. The stove in the kitchen has to be spotless, and all dishes must be washed, dried, and put away. This may not be exciting for your wife, but find your groove. Finding your groove is a journey, not a destination. It will change as you mature together. I love expressing myself in poetry. Here is a poem about my wife that I would like to share with you. (Maybe this will get me out of the next book that she writes . . .)

Loving Ramona

Loving Ramona is part of the reason that God Created me

Loving Ramona is my passion and drive.

Loving Ramona motivates me to become the man God called me to be

Loving Ramona causes me to share my love with her and not deprive

Loving Ramona I do not have anything to prove

Loving Ramona has led to our thirty-five-year Groove

On the next few pages, we would like to share with you keys to marriage from other married couples.

Keys to Marriage:

Nathaniel and Carolyn Stampley: married for forty-eight years

Peace be with you, and congratulations on the marriage and book. July 29th, 2020, we will celebrate forty-eight years. A successful and blessed marriage must be ordained by God and have effective communication, lots of patience, humor, trust, love, and a plan to succeed. Oh, it doesn't matter who has the final say, just as long as it is best for the marriage. God bless.

Rodney and Carol King: married for thirty-one years

We made thirty-one years on April 22nd. We started off as friends. Make sure you like the person you plan on spending the rest of your life with … and yes, the commitment is for life. Your fundamental values should be the same (equally yoked!) If there's something about them you don't like before you marry… it ain't gonna change once you say, "I do." Spoil your honey, and expect to be spoiled in return. Pick your battles… some aren't worth fighting. Always remember that you are a team, bookends, yin and yang, and peas in a pod!

Oscar & Carol Jones: married for thirty-four years

***Oscar T. Jones Jr.** Remember that your spouse is also your best friend. Establish and maintain great communication, never violate trust. Understand that the marriage has to have a business model to be successful. There are a lot of moving parts to maintain daily. You must respect and honor one another and establish a vision and mission statement as a guideline for a successful marriage. Leave your finances, planning, organizing, and management duties to the spouse with the better skill. Set an order to maintain peace and order in the household. Pray daily together for Gods covering and protection over yourselves, your family, your dreams, and desires with confidence and expectation. Understand that the trials and tribulations that come against your marriage and family will eventually pass. Give it to God with confidence that it's going to work in your favor. Lastly, remember Galatians 5:22. "But the Holy Spirit produces this kind of fruit in our lives: love, joy, peace, patience, kindness, goodness, faithfulness."

Also 1 Corinthians 13:4 "Love is patient and kind. Love is not jealous or boastful or proud. Remember, love keeps no record of wrong."

***Carol Jones.** Put God first, ourselves second. Then comes our children. Trust, forgiveness, unconditional love, keeping the flames alive when it comes to our intimacy, submission with respect, not keeping records of wrong, and sometimes having to be wrong when you are right are important. Laughter and serving in ministry together has kept Elder Oscar and I in the honeymoon phase for thirty-four years! We are called Team Jones because there is no *I* in team! He is the pen and I am his highlighter.

Michael and Charlotte Jones: married for five years

Congratulations, Mona, for completing your novel *Let's Stay 2gether*. You kept me waiting for a long time. I'm so happy you have completed your novel, and I'm confident it will bless others. A successful marriage requires real, honest communication. Communication is interactive, involving input from both individuals. A monologue is a one-way, single conversation that is heard with no response. I was married for twenty years, raised three kids, and thought I was in a marriage that would last a lifetime. Somewhere between careers and raising children, we lost real communication with each other. We were together and separated at the same time. After our youngest son completed high school and went off to college, the marriage was over. The lack of real communication ending our marriage was an unhealthy recipe to a successful marriage. God blessed me to remarry, and it will be five years on July 14, 2020. We pray together and are equally yoked. My healthy recipe for a successful marriage is prayer. My Dad's words of wisdom are "don't forget the family prayer."

Cliff and Rhonda Taylor: married for twenty-four years

Her Smith & Wesson 9mm has kept us together for twenty-four years

Richard and Carolyn Bryan: married for sixteen years

Sixteen years and counting What works for us is our 3 *C*'s. Just going to keep it 100. Communication, compromise, and counseling. This might not work for everyone, but for us, it definitely does.

Communication: There has to be a verbal line of communication between each other. The lack of it will lead to destruction. We have had moments where we have had to go to our separate corners/space from a heated moment to think about what was said and what the real problem was. We have learned that you can say something in a heated moment that you might regret later because you didn't think before you spoke. The tongue is sharper than any two-edged sword. Believe that. Words can definitely hurt. You can never take the words back because they have already been said and heard by each other. (*There is never any cussing involved just hurtful words.) I have even done the Whoopi Goldberg finger gesture to him from *The Color Purple* by saying "Ain't nothing good is going to come by you until you do right by me." Communicating with my spouse is so much better after we have had some time to reflect and have some downtime in our separate corners/space.

Compromise: We have learned in our relationship that we could agree to disagree with each other, but we had to learn to get to a neutral space where we could both agree to compromise about the broken situation to try to mend that situation back together. It's hard because I am stubborn at times because I am a control freak and a strong black superwoman that does everything for everybody, but I have learned to let him be the man that he is. I have had to scale back my control freak behaviors.

Counseling: We are never embarrassed to say that we have a marriage counselor. She has helped us through so many issues that have made us do some serious soul-searching between the two of us. Having a mediator to mediate issues that we couldn't see the light at the end of the tunnel made our marriage what it is now. We got the 3 *C*'s also from her. We got married having a blended family. Our kids were young at the time, so that in itself was challenging at times because of the different personalities. Now, all the kids are grown, and life is a lot easier, lol. Now, above all of this *God* was our #1 go-to. All I can say is prayer definitely changes things. I hope this is OK because I just wanted to be transparent and keep it real. Date night and getaways help as well. (Us time.)

Montely and Rachel Wilson-Bay: married for 10 years

Congrats, Ramona, on your book! To keep your marriage together as a married couple, have God as your core, communicate, make sacrifices, respect each other, and love one another.

Damon and Danyal (Dany) Collins: married for 6 years

We don't know if we have any real "secrets" to a happy marriage, but we know what works for us. We try to spend quality time together without the children; whether that means going out for date nights, or just relaxing with our favorite shows when the kids go to bed. We share some common interests, but we give each other the freedom and support to enjoy our individual interests and have our alone time. Lastly, we try not to let the little things get to us. We each have annoying little habits, but we love each other wholly and understand the bigger picture of who we are to each other.

Joseph (TMan) and Yolanda Caddell: married for 23 years

I know for sure just an open line of communication helps. I tell my husband that he can tell me anything and I will not judge him. So, if he feels overwhelmed, he will say it. We come up with a resolution. Or I may say, "Let's be friends today." Then, he will say, "I know you're married, but can we have lunch?" We do so many fun things.

Robert and Arleen LaVasser: married 10 years

The key to any long-term relationship in a marriage is trust; if you don't have trust, you don't have anything. You can't be on the front page of the book and your other half is in the back of the book. You both have to be in the middle of the book as one; that's the key to our relationship. We've been together for thirteen years and married ten years. This is the key to any long-term relationship.

Kenny and Patricia Ferguson: married for twenty-nine years

Girl, you know it takes putting God first, a lot of hard work, patience, perseverance, forgiveness, trust, loyalty, love, and not allowing the negativity of evil to be a partaker, for it will certainly take your marriage apart! It will be twenty-nine years August 25th!

Johnny and Karen Ray: married for ten years

What it takes for our marriage is a lot, a lot of prayer, a lot of compromise, and a lot of talking things out with each other... we have, in the early part of our marriage, had many unresolved issues, but we had to figure out that we were in it for the long haul; someone told us, "The vows say for better or worse, but they never said what the worst would be." So, when any couple takes those vows, there is no level of what your worse should be, and also have good married friends in your circle ones who will tell both of you when you are wrong or right and not take sides. We have couples in our circle that have twenty-five years, thirty years, and twenty-seven years together. It helps that we are the young ones, and last, we keep God first in our lives. We will have ten years of marriage behind us on September 5th of this year.

Michael and Vicky Allen: married for twenty-three years

When Michael and I began discussing the glue that has held us together. Michael brought up love, communication, trust, patience, tolerance, and always remembering our wedding vows. Every time we have the discussion regarding the "glue" that binds us together we can sum it up to one word. That word is love. Love is at the foundation on which our marriage stands. Without love all our heartfelt and difficult communications would cease. Because of our love we trust each other in every area of our marriage. We trust each other to remain faithful, we trust each other with our finances, our hopes and dreams. Love causes us to be patient and tolerant of one another, always finding ways to understand each other. To this day we still honor the vow that we pledged to God and to each other. Our love for God and for each other causes us to honor what we vowed twenty-three years ago. The blessing is we love each other more today than yesterday

Melvin and Julia Boyland: married for forty-two years

My philosophy is "Get it right before night." Keep the line of communication open. Pick the right time to discuss what bothers you. Love and communication go hand in hand. You can't have one without the other. That has kept us going for forty-two years. I can go on and on, but you didn't ask me to write the book. Oh, and make sure you don't leave prayer out.

Larry and Mary Nickerson: married for twenty-two years

As a single woman, I prayed and asked the Lord for a husband. He gave me His man that He chose for me. I honored the Lords decision and accepted the husband sent to me. I honored the vow I made before God to my husband. We have been tested in every situation, but as my husband follows Christ I follow him. Prayer is what kept us throughout the years.

Brian and Nyree Woods: married for three years

We have been married for three years. We have dated off and on for twenty-three years. For us to stay together, it takes a lot of remembrance. We remember what brought us together in the first place. There was a time when we were on our final hour; We were done. This ain't working! What we finally realized is every couple goes through tough times. You take the good with the bad. You have to have a "why." Why do I want my marriage to work? My husband and I share the same why. In addition to just loving each other to no end, we love being a family. We love that in a world where half of marriages end in divorce, we are giving our children a two-parent household. We fight hard, but we love harder. In the aftermath of the disagreements, I still see my husband as this beautiful soul. He is still the most attractive man to me, and I still love making love to him. Our intimacy is also our glue and a very important part of our relationship. Intimacy and laughter helps to settle our disputes and keep us going.

Kelly and Yvonne Perry: married for 23 years

Loving each other and understanding each other's ways, and even some of each other's irritating habits are important. Open communication is essential. Being open and honest, having trust, showing respect and appreciation for each other, and talking about the good and not so good moments of the marriage are also needed. Saying thank you or not being afraid to say you're sorry after a disagreement and sometimes compromising your needs for the other are essential. Continuing to enjoy each other's company, even in silence, while surfing the web or on the sofa watching a Netflix series is great. Keep intimacy alive… meaning not just sex, but holding hands, saying I love you, an unexpected hug or kiss on the cheek, pat on the butt, a foot or back rub, occasional cuddling (unless you're having a hot flash, then not!), etc. Date nights, day-outings, and laughter is important… being able to laugh with and at each other with no malice, knowing when to say something to your spouse about an issue and when not to open your mouth, and then later laughing about it is also a must.

Charles And Myrtle Jones: married for fifty years

A successful marriage entails living and being in "love with," the same person for a lifetime, which can only happen if God is the orchestrator of it all! First of all, when two "equally yoked," Christians marry, "God smiles." God approves of the marriage because they both have made the same commitment to him before the marriage even commences.

Even though God approves of the union from the beginning, the Christian couple has another requirement from God: to feed the spiritual side of them just as they're feeding the physical side of them. The couple nourishes their physical bodies with exercising, liquids, and nutritious diets daily for good health; conversely, the couple must feed the spiritual sides of themselves by reading the bible daily, having daily family prayer, attending bible study, Sunday School, and attending church on Sundays to ensure the spiritual side of them is growing and becoming healthy as well.

God knows that "spiritual growth," produces the "fruits of the spirit," such as being more patient, kind, loving, forgiving, understanding, and thoughtful. So, therefore, if a couple in their relationship with their spouse implements, these "fruits of the spirit" daily, can you imagine the positive effect on the marriage? Yes, it would be titled "A Successful Marriage in the Making!"

So, am I saying that it takes a commitment to our Lord and Savior Jesus Christ, first of all, for a couple to even have a chance at having a successful marriage, in addition to studying and growing spiritually as a couple daily? Yes, that's what I and my spouse of fifty years are saying. We married on August 8th, 1970, and on August the 8th of 2020, it will be fifty years; by the "Grace of God," we have had a successful Godly marriage for fifty years! We love God first, each other second, and we have cherished and adored each other the entire journey!

Hey, y'all. That's several years of marital wisdom. In the grand scheme of things, marriage is beautiful. It's two souls coming together to become one, through the good, the bad, and the ugly.

So, we leave you with let's love 2gether, let's pray 2gether, *let's play 2gether*. Three simple phrases easier said than done. But they will never work together if we don't try and stay 2gether. Sometimes, the roads are going to be rough, and the going is going to get tough. The hills will be hard to climb. But when we put God first all things are possible.

*After you have completed the book, please download the free workbook by clicking this link or entering http://letsstay2gether.com/Workbook

Thank you for taking the time to go through this marital groove with us. God Bless!